Plain and
Precious Things

Plain and Precious Things

Neal A. Maxwell

Deseret Book Company
Salt Lake City, Utah

Contents

Preface

This is *not* a Church publication, and the thoughts expressed herein do not necessarily represent the views of the First Presidency and the Council of the Twelve. The author, and he alone, is responsible for the content.

The entire royalties from this publication will be given to the Missionary Department of the Church for use in aiding in the distribution of the Book of Mormon, especially in those locations where the purchase of the book represents a sacrifice to the economically disadvantaged.

Acknowledgments

Once again, gratitude is given to friends who have been willing to peruse and comment, helpfully, on this manuscript concerning "plain and precious things."

Jeffrey Holland, Bruce Hafen, Jay Todd, and Elizabeth Haglund have generously so served as to format and structure.

Robert J. Matthews, Roy W. Doxey, and Daniel H. Ludlow made specific suggestions that have added to the substance of this volume.

To all of them, I give my deep appreciation. The gems from the scriptures noted herein deserved more polish—but such as there is is attributable to the above friends.

Jeananne Hornbarger has surely done her share, and my thanks go gladly and especially to her.

Chapter 1

"These Last Records . . .
Shall Establish the Truth of the First"

In this effort to rejoice over the Book of Mormon and the "other books"* of companion scripture—each in terms of its great significance—there is no intention to lessen the rejoicing over the Holy Bible, an inspirational and blessed book with its own great and splendid qualities. Every year, in fact, should be "The Year of the Bible."

The Holy Bible and other books of scripture—the Book of Mormon, the Doctrine and Covenants, and the Pearl of Great Price, along with those verses of the Bible which were blessed by Joseph Smith's translation—are, however, companions in the eyes of the Lord. We should not view them differently. Therefore, we should rejoice in the fulfillment of this prophecy: "These last records . . . shall establish the truth of the first." (1 Nephi 13:40.)

In fact, this commentary is dedicated to demonstrating the richness to be found in the interlacing insights of all books of scripture. When running the fingers of the mind through the many jewels and gems of truth therein, one cannot resist, as is done herein, the holding up of at least a few of the many jewels —and exclaiming joyfully over them. Along with the Holy Bible, these other books of scripture (see 1 Nephi 13:39) are

---

*In this volume, the phrases "other books" and "these last records" (see 1 Nephi 13:39-40) are to be understood as referring to the Book of Mormon, the Doctrine and Covenants, the Pearl of Great Price, and verses in the Bible that were revised in the Joseph Smith Translation (JST). Hereafter, these latter-day scriptures will be called the "other books."

truly a treasure trove, and any one of the jewels contained therein might be exclaimed over with equal enthusiasm.

Likewise, in writing a commentary, such as this volume, about any book of scripture, the author gladly acknowledges that there is no substitute for the real thing—reading the holy scriptures themselves. It was well said of the Bible: "Coming to [the Bible] through commentaries is much like looking at a landscape through garret windows over which generations of unmolested spiders have spun their webs." (Henry Ward Beecher.)

Throughout these books of scriptures, we see the summational and recurring themes that dominate in the Lord's declarations given in various dispensations. He is not random in His observations; He keeps them focused on the things that matter most—for which we should be everlastingly grateful.

These cumulative declarations thus form a broad and deep doctrinal delta, a rich and nourishing layer of spiritual soil laid down by God in which discipleship can become grounded, rooted, settled, and established. (See Ephesians 3:17; Colossians 1:23; 2:7; 1 Peter 5:10.)

Inevitably, it is the very doctrinal and spiritual content of these other books of scripture that one marvels and rejoices over. The structure, setting, and plot of the Book of Mormon, for instance, are interesting—much more complex and instructive than casual readers imagine as to style, form, and symbolism. But even so, by divine design such features are secondary to the book's major theme and messages.

The richness of the Book of Mormon is basically spiritual, not historical. It is one thing to focus on stage and scenery and quite another to focus on substance. The spiritual dimensions of this book of scripture are what this present volume focuses on. How reassuring and reverberating are its teachings about Jesus and the promises, perils, and purposes of this mortal life. And how real the perils in this earthly probation!

The other books of scriptures are not to be taken for

granted. They represent more than the giving of added aphorisms. Separate but interwoven, they come from the same Divine Source, and at a time when the New Testament needs and deserves support in declaring convincingly the divinity of Jesus. These reinforcing scriptures restore some of the "plain and precious things" previously lost. (1 Nephi 13:28.) The Lord Himself has declared these things as "plain and pure, and most precious" (1 Nephi 14:23); they arrive at a time in human history when there is so much preoccupation with transitory things that are filthy, obscure, and worthless.

Even so, it is easy, if one is not truly careful, to slide passively over the surface of the other books of scripture instead of pausing and pondering. It is so easy to scan rather than search the holy scriptures, and to nibble at them rather than to feast upon them! (See John 5:39; 2 Nephi 31:20.) For example, as one feasts upon the Book of Mormon, its conscientious and careful preparation is obvious. The caveats and counsel of its authors and editors become very apparent. Conscious of their own imperfections, they indicated no less than four times their concern lest their central message be obscured by their imperfections. Such careful and concerned preparation should be matched by careful and thoughtful reading.

The concluding lines of the title page of the Book of Mormon read, "And now, if there are faults they are the mistakes of men; wherefore, condemn not the things of God, that ye may be found spotless at the judgment-seat of Christ." Likewise we read these comments:

> If there be faults they be the faults of a man. But behold, we know no fault; nevertheless God knoweth all things; therefore, he that condemneth, let him be aware lest he shall be in danger of hell fire. (Mormon 8:17.)

> Condemn me not because of mine imperfection, neither my father, because of his imperfection, neither them who have written before him; but rather give thanks unto God that he hath made manifest unto you

our imperfections, that ye may learn to be more wise than we have
been. (Mormon 9:31.)

> Lord, the Gentiles will mock at these things, because of our
> weakness in writing; for Lord thou hast made us mighty in word by
> faith, but thou hast not made us mighty in writing; for thou hast made
> all this people that they could speak much, because of the Holy Ghost
> which thou hast given them. (Ether 12:23.)

These concerns are noted not because of any array of
imperfections in the Book of Mormon, but rather to show the
conscientiousness of the dedicated writers and editors who
with blood, sweat, and tears bequeathed the Book of Mormon
to all mankind.

It is the author's opinion that all the scriptures, including
the Book of Mormon, will remain in the realm of faith. Science
will not be able to prove or disprove holy writ. However,
enough plausible evidence will come forth to prevent scoffers
from having a field day, but not enough to remove the requirement of faith. Believers must be patient during such unfolding.
Besides, one can establish the authenticity of a Pauline epistle
and still refuse to heed the validity of its witness for Christ.

Writers and editors of the Book of Mormon repeatedly
indicated the selectivity used in choosing, under the inspiration
of heaven, what to include in that precious volume. It is understandable that some scholars would like even more contextual
material about the life, times, and culture of the peoples in the
Book of Mormon. Yet such attending history (of which there is
much more than we have been able to assimilate and
appreciate thus far[1]) is not the purpose for which the book has
been brought forward, as is indicated very early in the book
itself: "Wherefore, the things which are pleasing unto the world
I do not write, but the things which are pleasing unto God and
unto those who are not of the world." (1 Nephi 6:5.) While
these added scriptures fail to please the world, they are for
those who are in the world but not of the world.

We see an interesting mixture of author anxiety and selectivity in the following verse: "Nevertheless, I do not write anything upon plates save it be that I think it be sacred. And now, if I do err, even did they err of old; not that I would excuse myself because of other men, but because of the weakness which is in me, according to the flesh, I would excuse myself." (1 Nephi 19:6.)

The prophet Nephi later added another caveat: "And I engraved that which is pleasing unto God. And if my people are pleased with the things of God they will be pleased with mine engravings which are upon these plates." (2 Nephi 5:32.)

Perhaps there are still other purposes at work in the process of selectivity. In Third Nephi we read: "If it so be that they will not believe these things, then shall the greater things be withheld from them, unto their condemnation. Behold, I was about to write them, all which were engraven upon the plates of Nephi, but the Lord forbade it, saying: I will try the faith of my people." (3 Nephi 26:10-11.)

In any case, the other records, which remain unbequeathed and untranslated, focused on "the more particular part of the history" of the Lord's people. (2 Nephi 5:33.) Better a few more verses concerning the reality of the Resurrection than a few more concerning kingly succession. Therefore, we do not have "a hundredth part of the proceedings of this people." (Jacob 3:13.)

The chief editor, Mormon, provided parallel indications of the selectivity represented in the Book of Mormon: "The things which are upon these plates pleasing me, because of the prophecies of the coming of Christ." (Words of Mormon 1:4.) He then expressed the hope that his son Moroni would have an opportunity—not to expand further on military campaigns, but to "write somewhat" more "concerning Christ." (Words of Mormon 1:2.)

Thanks be to God, therefore, for all the pages of holy scripture! Praise be to the Father for the confirming scriptural witnesses and testaments of the divine mission of His Only Begotten Son, Jesus Christ! And thanks be for the elaborating, reinforcing, and clarifying content of these added books of scripture brought forth in this the last dispensation!

Let us rejoice as we read all holy writ—the Bible, the Book of Mormon, the Doctrine and Covenants, the Pearl of Great Price, the Joseph Smith Translation—which thus far constitute the "other books" of latter-day scripture. Let us give everlasting appreciation for the writers, editors, preservers, and translators who have done their work so well, all to the end that we might know of and believe in God's purposes for mankind, at the center of which is our Savior, His atonement, and His plain, precious, and redemptive gospel.

Note

1. Professor Gordon C. Thomasson of Brigham Young University has concluded that "more than twenty texts, types of texts, including whole documentary traditions, and oral sources" are referred to in the Book of Mosiah alone! This indicates a complexity of sources of content scarcely manageable except under the inspiration of heaven.

Chapter 2

The Convincing Role
of the "Other Books"

Twenty-five long centuries ago, an angelic visitor described and a prophet foresaw (in considerable detail) the coming forth of other books of scripture, particularly the Book of Mormon:

> And after . . . I beheld other books, which came forth by the power of the Lamb, from the Gentiles unto them, unto the convincing of the Gentiles and the remnant of the seed of my brethren, and also the Jews who were scattered upon all the face of the earth, that the records of the prophets and of the twelve apostles of the Lamb are true.
>
> And the angel spake unto me, saying: These last records . . . shall establish the truth of the first, which are of the twelve apostles of the Lamb, and shall make known the plain and precious things which have been taken away from them; and shall make known to all kindreds, tongues, and people, that the Lamb of God is the Son of the Eternal Father, and the Savior of the world; and that all men must come unto him, or they cannot be saved. (1 Nephi 13:39-40.)

In words laden with significance but too little pondered, Nephi says that "these *last* records," especially the Book of Mormon, will "establish the truth of the *first*," meaning the New Testament witness of Jesus Christ given by the Twelve Apostles. (1 Nephi 13:23, 40.) By divine decree, the timing of this corroboration was to occur when many of "the children of men shall esteem" Mosaic scripture (the first books of the Old Testament) "as naught." (Moses 1:41.) It was likewise timed to aid those in the gentile world who "stumble exceedingly" because of some "plain and precious" scriptures that are missing from the Bible. (1 Nephi 13:34; 14:1.)

God, who knew all things "from the beginning" (1 Nephi 9:6), also knew precisely when the blessed Bible's especial companion, the Book of Mormon, needed to arrive fresh for the fray, "proving to the world that the holy scriptures are true, and that God does inspire men and call them to his holy work in this age and generation, as well as in generations of old." (D&C 20:11.) How grateful we should be for the priceless Holy Bible, but no less so for precious and complementary latter-day scriptures in their contributions to a fulness of understanding.

Thus the "other books" of scripture happily provide, to all who will heed, multiple witnesses to the major message that Jesus of Nazareth, the Lamb of God, "is the Son of the Eternal Father, and the Savior of the world." (1 Nephi 13:40.)

What a marvelous and much-needed latter-day message has thus come forth, and in clear fulfillment of such sweeping declarations of divine intent. Truly, "there is nothing that the Lord . . . shall take in his heart to do but what he will do it." (Abraham 3:17.)

Among the many precious things given to us in the Book of Mormon are two forecasting verses, each with its special insights. The unfortunate mortal reaction to the Messiah in the meridian of time was not unexpected. Each of these verses was given, by revelation, centuries before Christ's first advent and His subsequent rejection by mortals living then:

> And the world, because of their iniquity, shall judge him to be a thing of naught; wherefore they scourge him, and he suffereth it; and they smite him, and he suffereth it. Yea, they spit upon him, and he suffereth it, because of his loving kindness and his long-suffering towards the children of men. (1 Nephi 19:9.)

> And lo, he cometh unto his own, that salvation might come unto the children of men even through faith on his name; and even after all this they shall consider him a man, and say that he hath a devil, and shall scourge him, and shall crucify him. (Mosiah 3:9.)

What sad words: "and even after all this they shall consider him a man." Yet is not that same challenge with us today? Many still judge Jesus to be a mere man and "to be a thing of naught." As an insightful author has observed, Christianity now struggles for a serious "hearing in a world where most would regard it not as untrue or even as unthinkable, but simply as irrelevant."[1]

How vital and timely, therefore, that other books of scripture should come forward attesting to His Lordship. There should be little puzzlement as to why the adversary seeks to demean or diminish the influence of these latter-day scriptures—scriptures that clearly establish the Lordship of Him whom the adversary sought to depose. There is wonderment, however, as to why some professed believers in Christ resent the coming forth of other books of Christocentric scripture.[2]

As the Lord declared, those who smugly say, "We have got a Bible, and we need no more Bible," fail to thank the Jews for the Bible. They forget, too, that "there are more nations than one." Why should people murmur because they receive more of His word?[3] (See 2 Nephi 29.) In a world in which more and more mortals, including those in so-called Christian nations, consider Jesus a mere man, is help needed or not? Jesus repudiated the provincialism of ancient Jews for touting Abraham as their father, when "of these stones" God could "raise up" children unto Abraham (see Matthew 3:9); in our time Christ renounced the insularity of those who scorn His power to "raise up" additional scripture!

Significantly, the angel who appeared so long ago to Nephi used the word *convincing* to describe the reinforcing role of these additional scriptures. (1 Nephi 13:39.) Likewise, Joseph in Egypt was told by the Lord how one of his modern seed, also to be named Joseph, would later bring forth the Lord's word to the ancient Joseph's seed "to the *convincing* them of my word." (2 Nephi 3:11. Italics added.) On the title page of the Book of

Mormon, the same word is used in the inspired declaration of the book's purpose: "to the *convincing* of the Jew and Gentile that Jesus is the Christ." Still later Nephi also used that very same word. (See 2 Nephi 25:18.) Moreover, the "convincing" of the Jews concerning Jesus' Messiahship is surely one of the Lord's priority purposes in the latter days. (See 2 Nephi 26:12.) Those who have given us the Book of Mormon never lost sight of this central purpose of convincing—nor should we. Moreover, the repeated use of that same, specific word is clearly not accidental.

To ponder how crucial the task of convincing both Jew and Gentile was—and is—we have only to recall Paul's lamentation how, to the Jew, Christ was a "stumblingblock," and to the Gentile, "foolishness." (1 Corinthians 1:23.) John, too, recorded some of the uncertainty and confusion of people in his time concerning Christ during His mortal Messiahship:

> Many of the people therefore, when they heard this saying, said, Of a truth this is the Prophet.
>
> Others said, This is the Christ. But some said, Shall Christ come out of Galilee?
>
> Hath not the scripture said, That Christ cometh of the seed of David, and out of the town of Bethlehem, where David was?
>
> So there was a division among the people because of him. . . .
>
> They answered and said unto him, Art thou also of Galilee? Search, and look: for out of Galilee ariseth no prophet.
>
> And every man went unto his own house. (John 7:40-43, 52-53.)

In fact, John wrote his Gospel "that [we] might believe that Jesus is the Christ, the Son of God; and that believing [we] might have life through his name." (John 20:31.)

No wonder Jacob characterized that very myopia in the meridian of time as "looking beyond the mark"—when the mark was Christ!

But now the clarion confirmation is given concerning another testament of Jesus Christ, the Book of Mormon, the record of ancient Americans of Jacobian descent. This book, through those of gentile America, will go forth to the Jews of the latter days.

> Now these things are written unto the remnant of the house of Jacob; and they are written after this manner, because it is known of God that wickedness will not bring them forth unto them; and they are to be hid up unto the Lord that they may come forth in his own due time.
> And this is the commandment which I have received; and behold, they shall come forth according to the commandment of the Lord, when he shall see fit, in his wisdom.
> And behold, they shall go unto the unbelieving of the Jews; and for this intent shall they go—that they may be persuaded that Jesus is the Christ, the Son of the living God; that the Father may bring about, through his most Beloved, his great and eternal purpose, in restoring the Jews, or all the house of Israel, to the land of their inheritance, which the Lord their God hath given them, unto the fulfilling of his covenant;
> And also that the seed of this people may more fully believe his gospel, which shall go forth unto them from the Gentiles; for this people shall be scattered, and shall become a dark, a filthy, and a loathsome people, beyond the description of that which ever hath been amongst us, yea, even that which hath been among the Lamanites, and this because of their unbelief and idolatry. (Mormon 5:12-15.)

The passing of the centuries has not made the challenge of convincing mortals any easier. Only God could compare the degrees of difficulty as between believing in Christ to come or Christ who has come. However, the challenge has surely been very real in every dispensation and situation.

The angel who appeared (around 124 B.C.) to King Benjamin movingly and prophetically described the coming of Jesus and the performing of His mortal ministry, His miracles and His work among the children of men, and then the glorious but awful Atonement: "And lo, he shall suffer temptations, and pain of body, hunger, thirst, and fatigue, even more than man can suffer, except it be unto death; for behold, blood cometh from every pore, so great shall be his anguish for the wickedness and the abominations of his people." (Mosiah 3:7. See also Luke 22:44; D&C 19:18.)

Significantly, the very names of the Savior and his mother were given to King Benjamin: "And he shall be called Jesus Christ, the Son of God, the Father of heaven and earth, the Creator of all things from the beginning; and his mother shall be called Mary." The angel also advised King Benjamin that after all Jesus would do in the meridian of time, the people of that time would, alas, react in this manner: "They shall consider him a man, and say that he hath a devil, and shall scourge him, and shall crucify him." (Mosiah 3:8-9.)

Hence we recognize the vital and essential *oneness* of the witness of the New Testament and the Book of Mormon, each given in order that all kindreds, tongues, and people may understand, convincingly, God's purposes for mankind and the unique role our supernal Savior, Jesus Christ, plays therein: as humanity's Redeemer.

Moreover, still "other sheep," a third group—neither of Jerusalem nor the Americas—heard Jesus' voice and were visited by Him. (See 3 Nephi 16:1-4; 17:4; 18:27.) Will there be an additional or third group of convincing and witnessing scriptures? Yes! Will the lost Ten Tribes—those of ancient Israel who did not remain with Judah, as well as a portion of Benjamin—bring their own records and scriptures? Yes! And eventually, by three scriptural witnesses, the Messiahship of Jesus of Nazareth will be finally established.

> For behold, I shall speak unto the Jews and they shall write it; and I shall also speak unto the Nephites and they shall write it; and I shall also speak unto the other tribes of the house of Israel, which I have led away, and they shall write it; and I shall also speak unto all nations of the earth and they shall write it.
>
> And it shall come to pass that the Jews shall have the words of the Nephites, and the Nephites shall have the words of the Jews; and the

Nephites and the Jews shall have the words of the lost tribes of Israel; and the lost tribes of Israel shall have the words of the Nephites and the Jews. (2 Nephi 29:12-13.)

These records that are yet to come forth will focus, as do all the others, on the centrality of Christ, His atonement and resurrection, and God's unfolding purposes for man.

Believers in and students of the Book of Mormon regard such correlative relationships between ancient and modern scriptures as being just what they are: the latticework of the Lord, revelations coming from the same Divine Source. To such people it is no surprise, therefore, to see such multiple interweavings and such abundant cross-support among the various books of scripture.

These correlated interweavings should give pause even to near believers and disbelievers, as well as those for whom any explanation of the origins of the Book of Mormon will do— except the real one! The Lord Himself declared, in majestic simplicity, of His use of parallels and similarities, "I speak the same words unto one nation like unto another. And when the two nations shall run together the testimony of the two nations shall run together also." (2 Nephi 29:8.) Unsurprisingly, the words of Ezekiel are correlated fully with the words of Nephi as to the oneness of purpose of these modern and ancient records. (See Ezekiel 37:19; 1 Nephi 13:40-41.)

The Prophet Joseph Smith was bright but young and lacking in formal education (as his earlier difficulties with spelling indicate). However, he achieved his remarkable translation of the Book of Mormon in a scant number of weeks, during which he had also to attend to some of the usual chores and duties that go with everyday living. Such a compression of calendar days makes the remarkable correlation of so much significant material explainable in only one way—divine revelation. And with revelation comes the reemergence of plain and precious spiritual truths that were of more import than Joseph Smith could, at the time, fully appreciate.

Anyone who has done much reading finds himself grateful for books that contain two or three significant truths or great ideas. Sometimes we gladly settle for articulate restatement and rephrasings. Many books, though well-received, contain virtually nothing that is precious—no precious nuggets at all.

Thus the density of the spiritual truths of the Book of Mormon is especially impressive. Indeed, the doctrinal density of the Book of Mormon clearly overshadows the portion that is given over to history or to details such as the description of Nephite money. The book's structure is clearly and intentionally secondary to its substance, and its plot to its principles.[4] The Book of Mormon's innumerable insights and doctrinal declarations constitute their own witness. Clearly, this book came *through* but not *from* Joseph Smith. It is translated language, but its substance is of the Savior.

In varying degrees of clarity, the Psalmist, Isaiah, Enoch, and Moroni foretell how "these last records" were to emerge as "truth . . . out of the earth." (See Psalm 85:11; Isaiah 29:4; Moses 7:62; Mormon 8:16.)[5] But even the unusual and remarkable externals of the book's emergence are subsidiary to its fundamental purposes. The clear words of the Lord to Enoch confirm that the central purpose of the Book of Mormon would be "to bear testimony of mine Only Begotten; [and] his resurrection from the dead." (Moses 7:62.)

Moroni, so much of whose life was involved with the preparation, preservation, and coming forth of the Book of Mormon, declared that the whole process of the book's coming forth "shall be done by the power of God." He then added both a stern caveat and a splendid reassurance: "And he that shall breathe out wrath and strifes against the work of the Lord, and against the covenant people of the Lord who are the house of Israel, and shall say: We will destroy the work of the Lord . . . the same is in danger to be hewn down and cast into the fire; for the eternal purposes of the Lord shall roll on, until all his promises shall be fulfilled." (Mormon 8:16, 21-22.)

Those who seek to "destroy the work of the Lord" in any age are surely to be included in that circle of love which Jesus urged His disciples to have—even for their enemies. On occasion, however, such love can be properly expressed by warnings such as were given by Moroni. These sobering words from a latter-day prophet, Heber C. Kimball, are a modern counterpart: "God says judgment shall come, and it shall commence at the house of God first, and then it will come upon those that have rebelled in the house of God; and all of the suffering that ever fell upon men and women will fall upon the apostates. They have got to pay all the debt of the trouble that they have brought upon the innocent from the days of Joseph to this day, and they cannot get rid of it." (*Journal of Discourses* 5:94.)

Such warnings are stern, yet they represent one way of reaching out to a careless friend who is about to plunge heedlessly over a precipice. A strong, plain exhortation is necessary to warn him; a mere frown will not do.

Given such elaborate preparation and such correlation over the centuries, we should ponder the Lord's counsel given to Joseph Smith in July 1828. As the coming forth of "these last records," the Book of Mormon, at long last drew near in order to amplify "the knowledge of a Savior," the Lord declared:

> Nevertheless, my work shall go forth, for inasmuch as the knowledge of a Savior has come unto the world, through the testimony of the Jews, even so shall the knowledge of a Savior come unto my people. . . . And for this very purpose are these plates preserved, which contain these records . . . that they might know the promises of the Lord, and that they may believe the gospel and rely upon the merits of Jesus Christ. (D&C 3:16, 19-20.)

Just how interactive the Book of Mormon and the Bible are designed to be can be gauged in the juxtaposing of the two books, which represent the "this" (the Book of Mormon) and "that" (the Bible) in these verses:

> Therefore repent, and be baptized in the name of Jesus, and lay hold upon the gospel of Christ, which shall be set before you, not only in this record but also in the record which shall come unto the Gentiles from the Jews, which record shall come from the Gentiles unto you.
>
> For behold, *this* is written for the intent that ye may believe *that*; and if ye believe *that* ye will believe *this* also; and if ye believe *this* ye will know concerning your fathers, and also the marvelous works which were wrought by the power of God among them. (Mormon 7:8-9. Italics added.)

Thus so much has been done in order that mankind may have convincing words about Jesus. Confusion concerning the identity and reality of Christ and of God's purposes for the people of this planet can be disastrous to one's soul or a whole society. Jacob was given by an angel this sobering declaration about the perils of nonrecognition of the reality and identity of the Savior: "Wherefore, as I said unto you, it must needs be expedient that Christ—for in the last night the angel spake unto me that this should be his name—should come among the Jews, among those who are the more wicked part of the world; and they shall crucify him—for thus it behooveth our God, and there is none other nation on earth that would crucify their God." (2 Nephi 10:3.)

At least two times in Jesus' earthly ministry, the possibility that He was the expected Messiah was discounted by disbelievers, because the scriptures available to the Jews were assumed to be silent concerning a prophet's coming out of Galilee or Nazareth—only Bethlehem was cited. (Micah 5:2; Matthew 2:3-6; John 7:41, 52.) The Book of Mormon, however, makes it clear that Jesus' unfolding life would involve Nazareth. (1 Nephi 11:13.) Significantly, Matthew made reference to the prophecy concerning Jesus' being a Nazarene, but it is an apparent reference to a lost book of scripture. (Matthew 2:23.)

Professor Robert J. Matthews has noted this example of the added facts given to us in Joseph Smith's translation of the Bible:

> As recorded in the King James Version, wise men from the East inquired of Herod about the birth of the "King of the Jews." Consequently, Herod asked the scribes "where Christ should be born." He was told that it was written, "And thou Bethlehem, in the land of Juda, art not the least among the princes of Juda: for out of thee shall come a Governor, that shall rule my people Israel." (Matt. 2:2-6.)
>
> However, as given in the JST, the men from the East asked Herod a more searching question: "Where is *the child* that is born, *the Messiah* of the Jews?" (The Prophet's changes here and hereafter are highlighted by italics.) Herod was told by the scribes that the prophets had written, "And thou, Bethlehem, *which lieth* in the land of *Judea, in thee shall be born a prince, which* art not the least among the princes of *Judea;* for out of thee shall come the *Messiah, who* shall *save* my people Israel." (JST Matt. 3:6.)
>
> As presented in the JST, it is not Bethlehem, but Jesus who is the prince; and he is not simply a Governor come to rule, but the *Messiah* come to *save* Israel. Surely it was Jesus (and not Bethlehem) who was the prince, for he (and not the whole village) was to inherit the throne of David and rule Israel "with judgment and with justice . . . for ever," as recorded in Isaiah 9:6-7.[6]

Once again, we see underscored the importance of having mortals in all ages understand and rely upon all of the scriptural evidence regarding Jesus. We see also how valuable to all are the special witnesses of the Savior:

> And now I, Nephi, write more of the words of Isaiah, for my soul delighteth in his words. For I will liken his words unto my people, and I will send them forth unto all my children, for he verily saw my Redeemer, even as I have seen him.
>
> And my brother, Jacob, also has seen him as I have seen him; wherefore, I will send their words forth unto my children to prove unto

them that my words are true. Wherefore, by the words of three, God hath said, I will establish my word. Nevertheless, God sendeth more witnesses, and he proveth all his words. (2 Nephi 11:2-3.)

How unfortunate and unnecessary were the reactions of those among whom opinion was divided concerning the ministry of Jesus, and who, after their uncertainty, went to their own homes. (See John 7:52-53.) In contrast, those on the American continent who were privileged to be taught directly by the resurrected Jesus were asked by Him to go to their homes and ponder what He had taught them, to discuss it in their families, and then to return again on the morrow. (3 Nephi 17:3.)

One cannot help but wonder what might have happened if, when Herod inquired of the scripturalists of his time concerning Jesus, those advisers had had access to or understood the fulness of the scriptures. (See Matthew 2:3-6.)

Furthermore, it is not solely the reality of a living Christ we are to grasp, but also His expansive role. There is a clarity and specificity in the added scriptures in the Book of Mormon:

In the beginning was the Word, and the Word was with God, and the Word was God. The same was in the beginning with God. All things were made by him; and without him was not any thing made that was made. (John 1:1-3.)

Behold, I am Jesus Christ the Son of God. I created the heavens and the earth, and all things that in them are. I was with the Father from the beginning. I am in the Father, and the Father in me; and in me hath the Father glorified his name. (3 Nephi 9:15.)

Likewise, not only do the additional scriptures *confirm* the reality of Jesus, but also a deepened *appreciation* emerges as one sees more clearly His unique and redemptive role, such as is seen in comparing these companion verses so moving and inspiring in their message to mortals:

Father, if thou be willing, remove this cup from me: nevertheless not my will, but thine, be done.

And there appeared an angel unto him from heaven, strengthening him.

And being in an agony he prayed more earnestly: and his sweat was as it were great drops of blood falling down to the ground. (Luke 22:42-44.)

For behold, I, God, have suffered these things for all, that they might not suffer if they would repent;

But if they would not repent they must suffer even as I;

Which suffering caused myself, even God, the greatest of all, to tremble because of pain, and to bleed at every pore, and to suffer both body and spirit—and would that I might not drink the bitter cup, and shrink—

Nevertheless, glory be to the Father, and I partook and finished my preparations unto the children of men. (D&C 19:16-19.)

And lo, he shall suffer temptations, and pain of body, hunger, thirst, and fatigue, even more than man can suffer, except it be unto death; for behold, blood cometh from every pore, so great shall be his anguish for the wickedness and the abominations of his people. (Mosiah 3:7.)

Moreover, the obedience of Jesus at Gethsemane reflected an obedience that was in place long before that agonizing moment: "But, behold, my Beloved Son, which was my Beloved and Chosen from the beginning, said unto me—Father, thy will be done, and the glory be thine forever." (Moses 4:2.)

Thus the Savior Himself, in these "other books" of modern scripture, has spoken in the first person, authenticating the manner in which He suffered while bringing about the atonement of mankind. He Himself reports on His agony. How marvelous and wondrous!

Jesus' modern revelations personalize His atonement, making abundantly clear what He so generously did for you and me. For some, the Christian religion can seem too removed or too abstract, and it is too much viewed as a "take it or leave it" part of life. There can be no such equivocating, however, if one ponders what modern revelation provides firsthand about the Master, with its many implications for each of us.

The elaboration and clarification of events yet future is no less evident than of matters past and present. One striking example concerns the dramatic and impending appearance of the resurrected Jesus to the Jews at the time of His second coming. This unusual scenario of delayed, then sudden, recognition (and then of deep regret) appears in the inspired writings of Zechariah:

> And I will pour upon the house of David, and upon the inhabitants of Jerusalem, the spirit of grace and of supplications: and they shall look upon me whom they have pierced, and they shall mourn for him, as one mourneth for his only son, and shall be in bitterness for him, as one that is in bitterness for his firstborn. (Zechariah 12:10.)

> And one shall say unto him, What are these wounds in thine hands? Then he shall answer, Those with which I was wounded in the house of my friends. (Zechariah 13:6.)

But notice the amplifying power—and likewise, its Christo-clarity—in the elaboration in modern scriptures:

Then shall the arm of the Lord fall upon the nations.

And then shall the Lord set his foot upon this mount, and it shall cleave in twain, and the earth shall tremble, and reel to and fro, and the heavens also shall shake.

And the Lord shall utter his voice, and all the ends of the earth shall hear it; and the nations of the earth shall mourn, and they that have laughed shall see their folly.

And calamity shall cover the mocker, and the scorner shall be consumed; and they that have watched for iniquity shall be hewn down and cast into the fire.

And then shall the Jews look upon me and say: What are these wounds in thine hands and in thy feet?

Then shall they know that I am the Lord; for I will say unto them: These wounds are the wounds with which I was wounded in the house of my friends. I am he who was lifted up. I am Jesus that was crucified. I am the Son of God.

And then shall they weep because of their iniquities; then shall they lament because they persecuted their king. (D&C 45:47-53.)

How stunning is this scene that is yet to be!

Furthermore, events past are shown more clearly to be Christocentric. Augmenting the verses in the Holy Bible, the Book of Mormon and the other books of modern scripture provide helpful elaboration that aids us not only in understanding more of what happened anciently, but also why, and its significance for us. Note how the writings of Moses and John in the following verses are clarified by the words of Nephi and Alma:

And the Lord sent fiery serpents among the people, and they bit the people; and much people of Israel died.

And the Lord said unto Moses, Make thee a fiery serpent, and set it upon a pole: and it shall come to pass, that every one that is bitten, when he looketh upon it, shall live.

And Moses made a serpent of brass, and put it upon a pole, and it came to pass, that if a serpent had bitten any man, when he beheld the serpent of brass, he lived. (Numbers 21:6, 8-9.)

And as Moses lifted up the serpent in the wilderness, even so must the Son of man be lifted up:

That whosoever believeth in him should not perish, but have eternal life. (John 3:14-15.)

And he did straiten them in the wilderness with his rod; for they hardened their hearts, even as ye have; and the Lord straitened them because of their iniquity. He sent fiery flying serpents among them; and after they were bitten he prepared a way that they might be healed; and the labor which they had to perform was to look; and because of the simpleness of the way, or the easiness of it, there were many who perished. (1 Nephi 17:41.)

Behold, he was spoken of by Moses; yea, and behold a type was raised up in the wilderness, that whosoever would look upon it might live. And many did look and live. (Alma 33:19.)

Divinely deliberate and serious symbolism is involved. Without this needed elaboration, the Old Testament episode of the fiery serpents does not give us a fulness of spiritual insight that can clearly be "for our profit and learning." (1 Nephi 19:23.) The symbolic emphasis in this episode is upon both the necessity and the simpleness of the way of the Lord Jesus. Ironically, in Moses' time many perished anyway. The promise for the future is as follows: "And as many as should look upon that serpent should live, even so as many as should look upon the Son of God with faith, having a contrite spirit, might live, even unto that life which is eternal." (Helaman 8:15. See also 1 Nephi 17:41; Alma 37:46.)

Thus, now we have the verified and amplified analogy, thanks to the precious and plain things given to us in "these last records."

The whole episode points toward the need to look upon Jesus Christ as our Lord, likewise a simple but unwaivable requirement. How plain and precious in any age! Yet believing in Jesus is sometimes regarded as foolishness. One can imagine the scoffing comments of some in Moses' time concerning the illogicality and foolishness of looking upon a brass pole in order to be healed and saved.

In the Book of Mormon we also receive some accompanying and fascinating insights into the relationship of the law of Moses and the gospel of Jesus Christ, as in these verses:

> And, notwithstanding we believe in Christ, we keep the law of Moses, and look forward with steadfastness unto Christ, until the law shall be fulfilled. . . .
>
> And we talk of Christ, we rejoice in Christ, we preach of Christ, we prophesy of Christ, and we write according to our prophecies, that our children may know to what source they may look for a remission of their sins. (2 Nephi 25:24, 26.)
>
> Now they did not suppose that salvation came by the law of Moses; but the law of Moses did serve to strengthen their faith in Christ; and thus they did retain a hope through faith, unto eternal salvation, relying upon the spirit of prophecy, which spake of those things to come. (Alma 25:16.)

The specific name of Jesus Christ does not appear in what has come forward as the Old Testament. (See Moses 1:41.) Paul, speaking of Moses' time, said this:

> By faith Moses, when he was come to years, refused to be called the son of Pharaoh's daughter;
>
> Choosing rather to suffer affliction with the people of God, than to enjoy the pleasures of sin for a season;
>
> Esteeming the reproach of Christ greater riches than the treasures of Egypt: for he had respect unto the recompence of the reward. (Hebrews 11:24-26.)

Moses' devotion to Jesus was not unique, as is shown in these confirming verses:

> For, for this intent have we written these things, that they may know that we knew of Christ, and we had a hope of his glory many hundred years before his coming; and not only we ourselves had a hope of his glory, but also all the holy prophets which were before us.
>
> Behold, they believed in Christ and worshiped the Father in his name, and also we worship the Father in his name. And for this intent we keep the law of Moses, it pointing our souls to him; and for this

cause it is sanctified unto us for righteousness, even as it was accounted
unto Abraham in the wilderness to be obedient unto the commands of
God in offering up his son Isaac, which is a similitude of God and his
Only Begotten Son. (Jacob 4:4-5.)

Since the Book of Mormon is to come forward to the convincing of the Jew that Jesus is the Christ, its careful attention
to the foreshadowing law of Moses will one day bring
considerable fruit among the children of Judah:

> Therefore, it is expedient that there should be a great and last
> sacrifice; and then shall there be, or it is expedient there should be, a
> stop to the shedding of blood; then shall the law of Moses be fulfilled;
> yea, it shall be all fulfilled, every jot and tittle, and none shall have
> passed away.
>
> And behold, this is the whole meaning of the law, every whit
> pointing to that great and last sacrifice; and that great and last sacrifice
> will be the Son of God, yea, infinite and eternal. (Alma 34:13-14. See
> 3 Nephi 15 for Jesus' declaration that the law of Moses is fulfilled in
> Him.)

Mankind also needs to be told (and is told even more
emphatically in latter-day scripture) about the terms of Jesus'
ransom of us from death, with the attendant accountability
that somberly rests upon us all.

> For behold, I, God, have suffered these things for all, that they
> might not suffer if they would repent;
>
> But if they would not repent they must suffer even as I;
>
> Which suffering caused myself, even God, the greatest of all, to
> tremble because of pain, and to bleed at every pore, and to suffer both
> body and spirit—and would that I might not drink the bitter cup, and
> shrink. (D&C 19:16-18.)

Even when the scriptures are so carefully assembled, there
are some, alas, who will "not search . . . nor understand great
knowledge." (2 Nephi 32:7.) The "great knowledge"—that
which stands highest in the hierarchy of truth—lies in the
realm of the spirit. It does not involve fleeting facts, but "the

deep things of God." (1 Corinthians 2:10.) Yet, in an incredible irony, such knowledge is regarded as foolishness by an exclusionary world. (See 1 Corinthians 1:23-26; 2:11-14; Jacob 4:13.) Such knowledge is not merely proximate information either—it is ultimate wisdom. (See 2 Nephi 9:28.)

The blessed Book of Mormon and "other books" provide not only the glorious confirmation of the central truths about man and the universe, but also much-needed elaboration and clarification about still other "plain and precious things"—the attendant truths so desperately needed by mankind as well. They are needed especially if we are to do what Nephi wisely did with holy scripture: "For I did liken all scriptures unto us, that it might be for our profit and learning." (1 Nephi 19:23.)

Just as some disbelievers are too casual in their approach to sense the self-confirming validity of the Book of Mormon, so some believers are too casual in their appreciation of added scripture, and thus fail to take the full measure of those plain and precious truths—truths "plain and pure, and most precious and easy to the understanding of all men" (1 Nephi 14:23)—which the Book of Mormon and other modern revelations supply and restore.

Often demonstrated in minute detail, the interlacing of these various books of scripture has been accomplished by a caring God, and with a precision made possible only through the correlating influence of His Holy Spirit.

Remarkable as young Joseph Smith was, translating the Book of Mormon without divine aid was beyond his ability and his perceptive powers. In the course of his translating and dictating various revelations, truths and concepts were passed through his mind, were struck off his vocal cords, and were transmitted by his tongue. Yet many of these were at that time beyond his ability to comprehend fully. Well might he have exclaimed, with both Job and the Psalmist, "Such knowledge is too wonderful for me; it is high, I cannot attain unto it."

(Psalm 139:6; Job 42:3.) We must not confuse, therefore, what is produced by mortals through deduction and induction with what is produced only by revelation.

It is surely no denigration to any prophet to indicate that he is weak and simple when compared with the Lord he serves. Certainly Joseph Smith saw himself this way. Even the Savior Himself said, "My doctrine is not mine, but his that sent me." (John 7:16.)

Granted, any powerful and profound truths that must be expressed in any mortal language or in translated language will shine that much less brightly than if rendered in the resplendent tongue of heaven.[7] But what we receive in the Book of Mormon is not simply the cumulative product of one or several bright minds, nor is it simply an accumulative array of expressions reflecting divine truths elsewhere encountered. The central and key expressions of these powerful and fundamental doctrines are revelation.

It is in that sense that the work of Joseph Smith clearly surpasses him. As it was with Nephi, so it was with Joseph: The key words "are the words of Christ, and he hath given them unto me." (2 Nephi 33:10.)

Periodic efforts to discount modern scripture vacillate in their focus, since disbelievers prefer any explanation to the real one. For instance, some critics compare the Book of Mormon to other books that have similarities in structure or rough parallels in plot. But this is like comparing a play empty of substance but using Shakespearean costumes with a genuine play of Shakespeare.

The interweavings of crucial insights in holy writ—even though subject to the imperfections of men—are impressive indeed. Textual truths show a focusing constancy, though recorded centuries apart. No wonder, for meager mortal minds need to see such focusing—there are already too many distractions. Likewise, the manner in which certain key points receive recurring emphasis is further affirmation of these truths.

Whatever the combination of individuals—Enoch, Moses, Nephi, Alma, Paul, Moroni, or Joseph—the link between them is clear. Each separate strand of prophetic utterance, though interwoven into a pattern of divine design, can be followed back to a single source, a loving Father whose central and grand declared purpose is to bring to pass the immortality and eternal life of man. (Moses 1:39.) All that Divinity does is, in fact, focused solely upon that which is "for the benefit of the world." (2 Nephi 26:24.) Has not the Psalmist said, "We are the people of his pasture, and the sheep of his hand"? (Psalm 95:7.) God has no distracting hobbies. While one's eye is to be single to His glory, we must remember that His glory is to bring to pass the immortality and eternal life of man.

In all this constancy, there is authenticity. Yet some would attempt to use the Lord's constancy against Him, denying to the latest prophet his sequential place in this unfolding but continuing pattern. Has not the adversary, however, always preferred to use the strategy of "heads I win, tails you lose," saying that if there is consistency, then the words have been copied; if there is inconsistency, they cannot both be true?

One can scarcely imagine, in fact, the adversary's failing to be very nervous indeed over the coming forth of "these last records" and other sacred records to testify to the divinity of our resurrected Lord. Him whom he once sought to displace, the adversary now seeks to diminish and to deny. (See Abraham 3:26-28.)

Such nervousness is certain to produce (as it has) frantic and clever efforts to deny, to discredit, to dissuade, and to divert as many mortals as possible from any of the holy scriptures. The tempter, of course, prefers no scriptures at all; next, only a few scriptures; and if people insist on reading, let it be superficially, occasionally, and only partially. Otherwise, the holy scriptures' anthem of affirmation, underscoring life's purpose, and their convincing chorus of confirmation of Christ will be heard by many and will be believed. And so will the other major messages contained in "these last records," which record the simplicity, the symmetry, and the Christocentricity of the holy scriptures, brought forth in our time by a gracious and generous God.

Notes

1. Penelope Fitzgerald, *The Knox Brothers* (New York: Coward, McCann & Geoghegan, Inc., 1977), p. 106.
2. Some form of Christ's name is mentioned on an average of every 1.7 verses of the Book of Mormon. (See Susan Ward Easton, "Names of Christ in the Book of Mormon," *Ensign*, July 1978, p. 61.)
3. As an articulate expression of this ingratitude, we have the words attributed to Lord Balfour concerning how the "Christian religion and civilization owe to Judaism an immeasurable debt, shamefully ill repaid." (Barbara Tuchman, *Proud Tower* [New York: Macmillan, 1966], p. 48.)
4. Nephi wrote that the Book of Mormon, once issued, was to be with mankind for a long time—"from generation to generation as long as the earth shall stand." (2 Nephi 25:22.)
5. See also Professor Keith Meservy's informative article, "Ezekiel's Sticks," *Ensign*, September 1977, pp. 22-27.
6. Robert J. Matthews, "A Greater Portrayal of the Master," *Ensign*, March 1983, p. 9.
7. "The Book of Mormon in no case contradicts the Bible. It has many words like those in the Bible, and as a whole is a strong witness to the Bible. Revelations, when they have passed from God to man, and from man into his written and printed language, cannot be said to be entirely perfect, though they may be as perfect as possible under the circumstances; they are perfect enough to answer the purposes of Heaven at this time." (Brigham Young, *Journal of Discourses* 9:310.)

Chapter 3

Major Messages of Modern Scripture

In the much-needed witness-bearing that the Book of Mormon provides conjointly with the apostolic witness given in the New Testament, Jesus' role as Redeemer is underscored time and time again. In addition to this *leitmotiv*, blessedly, so there is recurring reference to the reality of the resurrection from the dead. Speaking to Enoch, the Lord, the first fruits of the resurrection, declared how the Book of Mormon would also be a witness to His resurrection "from the dead; [but] also the resurrection of all men." (Moses 7:62.) One has only to reflect upon how he would feel if Jesus were the *only* fruits of the resurrection; the miracle of the resurrection would still be impressive, but too exclusive to offer the rest of us real hope.

As to the fundamental importance of the resurrection, we witness the resplendent correlating influence of the Spirit. In the New Testament we read that, after Jesus' resurrection, "many bodies of the Saints which slept arose, . . . and went into the holy city, and appeared unto many." (Matthew 27:52-53.) On the American continent, the same unprecedented events occurred, as prophesied by Samuel the Lamanite:

> And behold, there shall be great tempests, and there shall be many mountains laid low, like unto a valley, and there shall be many places which are now called valleys which shall become mountains, whose height is great.
>
> And many highways shall be broken up, and many cities shall become desolate.

And many graves shall be opened, and shall yield up many of their dead; and many saints shall appear unto many. (Helaman 14:23-25.)

The resurrected Jesus made a special point of ensuring that this glorious event—witnessed alike on two hemispheres, and in which all mortals have an inexpressibly important and personal stake—was likewise carefully recorded. In fact, Jesus, noting the neglect of Samuel's prophecy, commanded that it be written. (See 3 Nephi 23:9-11.) No wonder, for He anticipated the subsequent reactions to the reality of the resurrection, such as those of the Athenians to Paul's preaching: "And when they heard of the resurrection of the dead, some mocked: and others said, We will hear thee again of this matter." (Acts 17:32.)

Jesus, the Jehovah of the Old Testament (who had been so careful to see that much lesser facts were carefully established in the mouths of two or three witnesses), insisted that the two central facts of human history, the atonement and the resurrection, be carefully established in the pages of the two great written witnesses of Him and the resurrection.*

Such careful correlation and amplified attesting would surely not surprise previous prophets—nor should it us.

The above is not recited just to note how reassuringly tidy the restored gospel is, nor how impressively exacting about facts the Lord is. Instead, one should ask, "What knowledge does the world need to have more than the sure testimony and evidence that Jesus is the Christ and that His atonement actually accomplished God's great plan of redemption, whereby mankind will be blessed with immortality?" In a world filled increasingly with drift, disbelief, and despair, what more welcome "good news" could be given?

For many years now—in literature, film, and music—we have witnessed increasing expressions of a profound sense of

---

*And, happily, a third scriptural witness to the reality of the resurrection is yet to make its appearance. See pages 12-13 of this volume.

what has come to be called existential despair, a hopelessness beyond hope. Granted, the human scene also includes many people who go happily about life's labors untouched by these feelings. But holocausts and wars have taken their terrible toll of hope among twentieth-century man. Said one eminent scientist, "The most poignant problem of modern life is probably man's feeling that life has lost its significance . . . [a] view . . . no longer limited to the philosophical or literary *avant garde*. It is spreading to all social and economic groups and affects all manifestations of life."[1]

One need not question either the reluctance or the sincerity with which some despairing individuals have come to such false conclusions. In fact, one feels compassion and desires to reach out to them in genuine entreaty. And the glorious books of scripture do combine to reach out in shining hope to all mankind.

One recent television drama, its closing scene in a cemetery, conveyed well this confusion and purposelessness as a character lamented poignantly, "Are all men's lives . . . broken, tumultuous, agonized and unromantic, punctuated by screams, imbecilities, agonies and death? Who knows? . . . I don't know. . . . Why can't people have what they want? The things were all there to content everybody, yet everybody got the wrong thing. I don't know. It's beyond me. It's all darkness."[2]

But such poignancy is obviously no guarantee as to the accuracy of the perception. Moreover, in human affairs, erroneous and unchallenged assertions sometimes assume an undeserved aura of truth. While a modern scriptural response to this increasing hopelessness may not create conviction in all such disbelievers, it can bolster believers against the silent erosion of their convictions. Besides, as an ancient prophet observed, sadness and badness are mutually reinforcing, for "despair cometh because of iniquity." (Moroni 10:22.)

Thanks to the "plain and precious" scriptures, we can place such lamentations beside the revelations of God; the expressions of despair beside the divine annunciations of hope; the fears of extinction alongside the reassurances of the resurrection; the provincialism beside the universalism of the gospel of Jesus Christ. Then we see how myopic some mortals are—like absorbed children in a treehouse pretending they are brave and alone!

The lamentations: Man lives in "an unsponsored universe," a universe "without a master,"[3] which "cares nothing for [man's] hopes and fears," an "empire of chance" in which man falls victim to "the trampling march of unconscious power."[4]

The revelations:

God himself that formed the earth . . . created it not in vain, he formed it to be inhabited. (Isaiah 45:18.)

For he is our God; and we are the people of his pasture, and the sheep of his hand. (Psalm 95:7.)

For behold, this is my work and my glory—to bring to pass the immortality and eternal life of man. (Moses 1:39.)

Men are, that they might have joy. (2 Nephi 2:25.)

But the very hairs of your head are all numbered. (Matthew 10:29-30.)

But only an account of this earth, and the inhabitants thereof, give I unto you. For behold, there are many worlds that have passed away by the word of my power. And there are many that now stand, and innumerable are they unto man; but all things are numbered unto me, for they are mine and I know them. (Moses 1:35.)

The fears: Mankind is "destined to extinction. . . . There is nothing we can do." Also, "We have no personal life beyond the grave; / There is no God; Fate knows no wrath nor ruth."[5]

The reassurances:

And the graves were opened; and many bodies of the saints which slept arose, and came out of the graves after his resurrection, and went into the holy city, and appeared unto many. (Matthew 27:52-53. See also 3 Nephi 23:9-11.)

O death, where is thy sting? O grave, where is thy victory? (1 Corinthians 15:55.)

O how great the plan of our God! (2 Nephi 9:13.)

In order to alter attitudes and behavior, such glorious facts attested to by scripture must still be "mixed with faith," said Paul. (Hebrews 4:2.) Some who despair, as Peter said, "willingly are ignorant." (2 Peter 3:15.) And, wrote Paul, "The Jews require a sign, and the Greeks seek after wisdom." (1 Corinthians 1:22.) Or, as Nephi said, some will "not search . . . nor understand great knowledge." (2 Nephi 32:7.) For these a pessimistic philosophy is "pleasing unto the carnal mind." (Alma 30:53.) Why? Because behavioral permissiveness flourishes amid a sense of hopelessness. Because if human appetites are mistakenly viewed as the only authentic reality, and "now" as the only moment that matters, why should one inhibit any impulse or defer any gratification? Hence the importance of declarations as to how impending immortality and the fact of our personal accountability are inextricably intertwined.

The foregoing constitutes but one illustration of the transcendent importance of modern scriptures in (1) establishing the truth of the New Testament's apostolic witness for Jesus, (2) corroborating the reality of the glorious resurrection, and (3) verifying God's loving and redemptive purposes for mankind.

Surely it is glorious to know that our redemptive and selfless Lord "doeth not anything save it be for the benefit of the world." (2 Nephi 26:24.)

At another level of scriptural significance, one gratefully ponders Paul's reminding references to those who live without hope and "without God in the world." (Ephesians 2:12; 1 Thessalonians 4:5.) Observe what happens by way of expanding our perception when those excellent words of Paul are placed alongside these parallel words from the Book of Mormon:

> And now, my son, all men that are in a state of nature, or I would say, in a carnal state, are in the gall of bitterness and in the bonds of iniquity; they are without God in the world, and they have gone contrary to the nature of God; therefore, they are in a state contrary to the nature of happiness. (Alma 41:11.)

> Yea, every knee shall bow, and every tongue confess before him. Yea, even at the last day, when all men shall stand to be judged of him, then shall they confess that he is God; then shall they confess, who live without God in the world, that the judgment of an everlasting punishment is just upon them; and they shall quake, and tremble, and shrink beneath the glance of his all-searching eye. (Mosiah 27:31. See also Mosiah 16:1.)

Thus we see clearly that to live without God in the world is to live "in a state contrary to the nature of happiness." Yet, one day even those who have so existed (they can hardly be said to have "lived") will acknowledge the justice of God.

Perceptively and courageously, Aleksandr Solzhenitsyn declared that if he were asked to identify the principal trait of the twentieth century, it would be "men have forgotten God," a "determining factor in all the major crimes of this century."[6]

Little wonder that Joseph Smith—who, in the theophany of Palmyra, saw the Father and the Son and who helped to restore a more complete knowledge of God in the world—was so very firm in declaring, "Happiness is the object and design of our existence."[7] It is knowing the true nature of God and happiness and then applying "plain and precious" truths from God that makes human happiness possible on this planet—and subsequently!

How much difference it would make if those in the world who, at best, regard Jesus merely as a great moral teacher could accept these and other simple, plain, and yet profound scriptural declarations from Him and about Him and His gospel. His rescue mission to mortals is set forth so plainly:

Behold I have given unto you my gospel, and this is the gospel which I have given unto you—that I came into the world to do the will of my Father, because my Father sent me.

And my Father sent me that I might be lifted up upon the cross; and after that I had been lifted up upon the cross, that I might draw all men unto me, that as I have been lifted up by men even so should men be lifted up by the Father, to stand before me, to be judged of their works, whether they be good or whether they be evil—

And for this cause have I been lifted up; therefore, according to the power of the Father I will draw all men unto me, that they may be judged according to their works.

And it shall come to pass, that whoso repenteth and is baptized in my name shall be filled; and if he endureth to the end, behold, him will I hold guiltless before my Father at that day when I shall stand to judge the world.

And he that endureth not unto the end, the same is he that is also hewn down and cast into the fire, from whence they can no more return, because of the justice of the Father. . . .

And no unclean thing can enter into his kingdom; therefore nothing entereth into his rest save it be those who have washed their garments in my blood, because of their faith, and the repentance of all their sins, and their faithfulness unto the end.

Now this is the commandment: Repent, all ye ends of the earth, and come unto me and be baptized in my name, that ye may be sanctified by the reception of the Holy Ghost, that ye may stand spotless before me at the last day.

Verily, verily, I say unto you, this is my gospel; and ye know the things that ye must do in my church; for the works which ye have seen me do that shall ye also do; for that which ye have seen me do even that shall ye do;

Therefore, if ye do these things blessed are ye, for ye shall be lifted up at the last day. (3 Nephi 27:13-17, 19-22.)

The resurrected Savior has given us yet another summation of His gospel message. Significantly, He did this after citing, at length, the role of the Book of Mormon in the latter days:

The Book of Mormon . . . contains a record of a fallen people, and the fulness of the gospel of Jesus Christ to the Gentiles and to the Jews also;

Which was given by inspiration, and is confirmed to others by the ministering of angels, and is declared unto the world by them—

Proving to the world that the holy scriptures are true, and that God does inspire men and call them to his holy work in this age and generation, as well as in generations of old;

Thereby showing that he is the same God yesterday, today, and forever. . . .

And gave unto them commandments that they should love and serve him, the only living and true God, and that he should be the only being whom they should worship.

But by the transgression of these holy laws man became sensual and devilish, and became fallen man.

Wherefore, the Almighty God gave his Only Begotten Son, as it is written in those scriptures which have been given of him.

He suffered temptations but gave no heed unto them.

He was crucified, died, and rose again the third day;

And ascended into heaven, to sit down on the right hand of the Father, to reign with almighty power according to the will of the Father;

That as many as would believe and be baptized in his holy name, and endure in faith to the end, should be saved—

Not only those who believed after he came in the meridian of time, in the flesh, but all those from the beginning, even as many as were before he came, who believed in the words of the holy prophets, who spake as they were inspired by the gift of the Holy Ghost, who truly testified of him in all things, should have eternal life,

As well as those who should come after, who should believe in the gifts and callings of God by the Holy Ghost, which beareth record of the Father and of the Son;

Which Father, Son, and Holy Ghost are one God, infinite and eternal, without end. Amen.

And we know that all men must repent and believe on the name of Jesus Christ, and worship the Father in his name, and endure in faith on his name to the end, or they cannot be saved in the kingdom of God. (D&C 20:8-12, 19-29.)

We thus hear from Jesus Himself, simply and powerfully, the essence of His gospel, the distillation of His doctrines. We understand firsthand the nature of His simple but sublime rescue mission performed on this planet.

Alas, however, the Lord has declared in regard to the commitment of some humans to truth: "Behold, I say unto you, that they desire to know the truth in part, but not all, for they are not right before me and must needs repent." (D&C 49:2.)

If mortals accept only part of Jesus' glorious gospel, their deprivation and suffering are self-imposed. Yet God would have all mortals enjoy a fulness of fact as well as happiness. Therefore, the reality of resurrection in Jesus' gospel has received recurring emphasis throughout the various volumes of scriptures—and by divine instruction. Jacob, in fact, was told to "engraven the heads" of pivotal teachings on the precious plates. If necessary, he was to let other lesser items go. (See Jacob 1:1-4.)

Granted, many, if not most, mortals will reject both the validity and the simplicity of Christ's gospel message. What is difficult to comprehend, however, is that some would criticize His message because of its inviting simplicity. (See Jacob 4:14.)

It is in clustered verses such as those cited that we experience the Author of the Beatitudes telling us who He is and also about the required ordinances of His gospel. And there is no nonsense about His being merely a great moral teacher!

The disbelief that was present in dispensations past is unfortunately seen again in our time. As we read in 2 Chronicles, "They mocked the messengers of God, and despised his words, and misused his prophets, until the wrath of the Lord arose against his people, till there was no remedy." (2 Chronicles 36:16.)

Why is this so? Manipulation of human vanity by the miserable one is but one obvious explanation, as Nephi tells us: "O that cunning plan of the evil one! O the vainness, and the frailties, and the foolishness of men! When they are learned they think they are wise, and they hearken not unto the counsel of God, for they set it aside, supposing they know of themselves, wherefore, their wisdom is foolishness and it profiteth them not. And they shall perish." (2 Nephi 9:28.)

Moreover, we receive from Nephi very clear confirmation of Jesus' words to Nicodemus (see John 3:35): the ordinance of baptism and the bestowing of the gift of the Holy Ghost are *not* optional. Ponder this unequivocal elucidation:

> Know ye not that he was holy? But notwithstanding he being holy, he showeth unto the children of men that, according to the flesh he humbleth himself before the Father, and witnesseth unto the Father that he would be obedient unto him in keeping his commandments.
>
> Wherefore, after he was baptized with water the Holy Ghost descended upon him in the form of a dove.
>
> And again, it showeth unto the children of men the straitness of the path, and the narrowness of the gate, by which they should enter, he having set the example before them.
>
> And he said unto the children of men: Follow thou me. Wherefore, my beloved brethren, can we follow Jesus save we shall be willing to keep the commandments of the Father? (2 Nephi 31:7-10.)

For those who scoff at the need for ordinances or who merely regard these as discretionary niceties, the constancy and consistency of these interweavings of prophetic utterances are needed declarations. To avert one's gaze from the necessity of the required ordinances is to be in peril, in yet another way, of "looking beyond the mark." (Jacob 4:14.)

Interspersed with these major messages involving deep doctrines and truths of incredible importance are still other "plain and precious things" God would have us know and follow. Blessedly, the "other books" of scripture not only *inform* us, but also *inspire* us to savor these other truths that come to us without complexity. They are too precious to be enclosed in overmuch erudition, too laden with inspiration and direction to be expressed other than with concision.

Notes

1. R. Dubos, *So Human an Animal* (New York: Charles Scribner's Sons, 1968), pp. 14f.
2. *The Good Soldier*, Public Broadcasting Systems, 1983.

3. Albert Camus, *The Myth of Sisyphus and Other Essays* (New York: Vintage Books, 1959), pp. 90-91.
4. Bertrand Russell, "A Free Man's Worship," *Mysticism and Logic* (New York: Doubleday Anchor Books, 1957), pp. 43, 54.
5. James Thompson, *The City of Dreadful Night and Other Poems* (London: Bertram Dobell, 1899), pp. 29-30, 35-36.
6. Aleksandr Solzhenitsyn, *National Review*, July 22, 1983, p. 873.
7. *History of the Church* 5:134.

Chapter 4

Plain and Precious Things

In addition to the previously cited confirmation of the Christocentricity of the universe, one sees numerous examples of elaboration and clarification of other basic and important truths in the Book of Mormon and the other books of scripture. These, too, invite more careful consideration. These precious and plain truths are not mere footnotes. Instead, they are bolstering and guiding principles that can do so much to keep us mortals walking steadily on the strait and narrow path and from stumbling needlessly. (See 1 Nephi 13:34; 14:1.)

Likewise, the spiritual yield from these plain and precious truths can bring fresh cause to believe to those whose esteem for the Bible is, alas, diminished.

As Professor Robert Matthews has written, "One of the greatest contributions of latter-day revelation is that the Bible tells 'what,' whereas the Book of Mormon explains 'why' — why the fall, why the atonement, and so forth."[1]

These same added truths can further reinforce those whose esteem for the Holy Bible is already high and who will, therefore, rejoice sincerely at receiving another plain witness and testament of Jesus. (See Moses 1:41; 1 Nephi 13:40.)

Indeed, some of the power of the scriptures lies in their very plainness. G. K. Chesterton wrote well of the power of gospel plainness: "The grinding power of the plain words of the Gospel story is like the power of mill-stones, and those who can read them simply enough will feel as if rocks had been rolled upon them. Criticism is only words about words, and of what use are words about such words as these?"[2]

The plainness often focuses on central matters, such as the Lordship of Jesus. By way of example, one notes at the end of chapter two and the beginning of chapter three in the book of Matthew an obvious time gap. How the marvelous but plain words from the Joseph Smith Translation fill that void! This added information about Jesus increases our appreciation of Him, giving to us a more complete picture of His preparation for His unique mortal ministry:

> And it came to pass that Jesus grew up with his brethren, and waxed strong, and waited upon the Lord for the time of his ministry to come.
>
> And he served under his father, and he spake not as other men, neither could he be taught; for he needed not that any man should teach him.
>
> And after many years, the hour of his ministry drew nigh. (JST Matthew 3:24-26.)

With these words underscoring the source of Jesus' unparalleled tutoring, no wonder His teaching in the temple while yet a youth "astonished" His audience. In the Joseph Smith translation of these verses, we learn that the learned doctors "were hearing [Jesus], and asking him questions." (JST Luke 2:46-47.) Still later in His ministry, it is no wonder that those who sought to interrogate Him finally reached the point where no man "durst ask him any question." (Mark 12:34.) Had He been merely a brilliant mortal—taught solely by mere mortals, however bright—such contemporaries could have expected to engage Him and to interrogate Him successfully. However, Jesus received special tutoring. He told some, "The Son can do nothing of himself, but what he seeth the Father do: for what things soever he doeth, these also doeth the Son likewise." (John 5:19.)

Instructive examples thus appear not only with regard to Jesus' actuality, but also as to the perfection of His resplendent personality. For instance, as Joseph Smith translated the powerful words of Alma, there flowed forth a powerful confirmation of and elaboration of otherwise terse verses from Isaiah, Matthew, and Paul. (See Isaiah 53:4, 5; Matthew 8:17.)

Paul may well have written more about how Jesus developed His matchless empathy—by personal experience with temptations—but, happily, these verses survived: "For in that he himself hath suffered being tempted, he is able to succour them that are tempted." (Hebrews 2:18.) "For we have not an high priest which cannot be touched with the feeling of our infirmities; but was in all points tempted like as we are, yet without sin." (Hebrews 4:15. See also D&C 62:1.)

Thus, by His actual and personal experiences in the flesh, Jesus was perfected in His empathy with regard to temptation. Moreover, He knew far more temptations and in an intensity greater than we shall ever know, being tempted "in all points" and "according to the flesh." (Alma 7:13.)

But what of the awful consequences to us of surrendering to temptation as we sin? How could Jesus, who never sinned, really know these feelings firsthand and "according to the flesh"? Moreover, since He apparently was healthy, how could His empathy be perfect concerning our sicknesses? How could He know how to succor us in the midst of our afflictions?

We receive through Alma one of those "plain and precious things"—grand and answering truth: The marvelous atonement brought about not only immortality but also the final perfection of Jesus' empathic and helping capacity—not only as to His perfect, personal understanding of temptation, but also the consequences of sin, afflictions, and sickness. Thus He can succor us and truly have mercy for us. As one reads these next verses, he, with Nephi, could well declare, "O how great the plan of our God." (2 Nephi 9:13.)

> And he shall go forth, suffering pains and afflictions and temptations of every kind; and this that the word might be fulfilled

which saith he will take upon him the pains and the sicknesses of his
people.

And he will take upon him death, that he may loose the bands of
death which bind his people; and he will take upon him their infirmities,
that his bowels may be filled with mercy, according to the flesh, that he
may know according to the flesh how to succor his people according to
their infirmities. (Alma 7:11-12. See also Matthew 8:17; Isaiah 53:45;
Mosiah 14:4.)

There is no personal problem through which anyone has
passed or will pass but what Jesus understands profoundly,
perfectly, and personally. How consoling! How comforting!
How conducive to our deeper adoration of our Savior!

No wonder Jesus Himself encouraged us not to scan but to
"search the scriptures; for . . . they are they which testify" of
Him. (John 5:39.) In them we see His reassuring *reality*, but
also His unsurpassed *personality*. How blessed we are, therefore, to have additional scriptures that we can search and that
add abundant witness concerning Jesus and His reality as well
as His preeminent personality!

Moreover, it is only as we come to understand better the
role of adversity in Jesus' life that the role of adversity in our
own lives becomes more clear as well. We can better trust an
empathic God amid trial as we see the Lord's latticework in the
various declarations about adversity, all of which were guided
by Him.

Peter wrote, "Beloved, think it not strange concerning the
fiery trial which is to try you, as though some strange thing
happened unto you." (1 Peter 4:12.)

Moroni confirmed the need for our patience in adversity
and elaborated, "Dispute not because ye see not, for ye receive
no witness until after the trial of your faith." (Ether 12:6.)

Alma, too, spoke of life's wrenching trials even for the
faithful: "Nevertheless the Lord seeth fit to chasten his people;
yea, he trieth their patience and their faith." (Mosiah 23:21.)

King Benjamin confirmed God's tutorial activism, as the

loving and fully understanding Lord seeks to help us become "a saint through the atonement of Christ the Lord, and . . . as a child, submissive, meek, humble, patient, full of love, willing to submit to all things which the Lord seeth fit to inflict upon him, even as a child doth submit to his father." (Mosiah 3:19.)

As God's spirit children, we had best take full heed, therefore, about the place of righteous obedience in this mortal curriculum!

Little wonder, centuries later, that another prophet, Brigham Young, tutored (as were so many predecessors) by so much personal adversity, received this parallel revelation: "My people must be tried in all things, that they may be prepared to receive the glory that I have for them, even the glory of Zion; and he that will not bear chastisement is not worthy of my kingdom." (D&C 136:31.)

While the soul shivers upon reading such declarations of divine intent regarding our individual tutoring, are not such truths so very "plain"? Are they not so very "precious"? Do they not give us much-needed perspective amid this soul-stretching mortal experience? Indeed, where would we be without them? Do they not, irrevocably and reassuringly, help us to center upon the Savior, His reality, His personality, and His role? And likewise upon God's plan of redemption with its personalized promises and purposes—and its "brightness of hope"—for a darkened and despairing world?

Indeed, the Book of Mormon makes plain that the fall of Adam is a reality and not a myth. Further, it teaches that the atoning mission of Jesus Christ is inseparably connected with the fall of Adam, a connection not made fully plain in the Bible except by Paul.

Thanks be to God for "these last records"! Let the faithful hold fast to the word of God, for the unfolding and "eternal purposes of the Lord shall roll on, until all his promises shall be fulfilled" (Mormon 8:22)—not only His purposes and promises for all mankind, but for each of us personally.

As previously indicated, in these multiple books of scripture, there emerges not only confirmation but clarification concerning ultimate matters such as the reality of the resurrection. But in recognition of our need, we also receive proximate help from plain and precious truths essential to our daily living and working out our own salvation—such as how we are to view adversity. Note the inspired words of Paul and Moroni:

And lest I should be exalted above measure through the abundance of the revelations, there was given to me a thorn in the flesh, the messenger of Satan to buffet me, lest I should be exalted above measure.

For this thing I besought the Lord thrice, that it might depart from me.

And he said unto me, My grace is sufficient for thee: for my strength is made perfect in weakness. Most gladly therefore will I rather glory in my infirmities, that the power of Christ may rest upon me. (2 Corinthians 12:7-9.)

And when I had said this, the Lord spake unto me, saying: Fools mock, but they shall mourn; and my grace is sufficient for the meek, that they shall take no advantage of your weakness;

And if men come unto me I will show unto them their weakness. I give unto men weakness that they may be humble; and my grace is sufficient for all men that humble themselves before me; for if they humble themselves before me, and have faith in me, then will I make weak things become strong unto them." (Ether 12:26-27.)

It is in the elaboration above that we learn that God's grace is sufficient for the humble and meek—not for everybody. There is confirmation of, as well as elaboration concerning, Paul's intimation that certain weaknesses and afflictions can even become a strength, and that afflictions are often given to us to humble us. The parallels are profound, though the scriptures came into being dispensations and continents apart.

On those occasions when we may feel we cannot bear up under our heavy burdens, we can draw some comparative succor from these lines: "And it came to pass that I was overcome because of my afflictions, for I considered that mine afflictions were great above all, because of the destructions of my people, for I had beheld their fall." (1 Nephi 15:5.) A great but much-burdened prophet provincially but humanly regarded his afflictions as "great above all."

Elsewhere, we read of a prophet who wept over the condition of "his brethren." (Moses 7:44. See also Enos 1:13; Mormon 6:1.) A suffering and jailed Joseph Smith was told by Him who alone could make such comparisons:

> My son, peace be unto thy soul; thine adversity and thine afflictions shall be but a small moment;
>
> And then, if thou endure it well, God shall exalt thee on high; thou shalt triumph over all thy foes.
>
> Thy friends do stand by thee, and they shall hail thee again with warm hearts and friendly hands.
>
> Thou art not yet as Job; thy friends do not contend against thee, neither charge thee with transgression, as they did Job. (D&C 121:7-10.)

As additional scriptures tell us more and more about Jesus' sufferings, His words bring us special consolation and personalized perspective: "Know thou, my son, that all these things shall give thee experience, and shall be for thy good. The Son of Man hath descended below them all. Art thou greater than he?" (D&C 122:7-8.)

How essential, how "plain and precious," these things are as we pass through our own soul-stretching tutorials! Furthermore, as we thus strive to move along the strait and narrow path, modern scriptures have removed some unintended and needless stumbling blocks from that solitary and stern path.

Notes

1. Robert J. Matthews, personal letter to the author.
2. Richard L. Purtill, *C. S. Lewis's Case for the Christian Faith* (San Francisco: Harper & Row, 1981), p. 56.

Chapter 5

Removing Some Stumbling Blocks

Only in modern revelation does the reader receive a much-needed additional dimension about the petitionary prayers we mortals place before the Lord, even when these are placed before Him in faith and reasonable righteousness. The absence of such plainness has been a stumbling block to some, because when precious things "plain unto the understanding of the children of men" are lost, "an exceedingly great many do stumble." (1 Nephi 13:29.)

Those who lack, through no fault of their own, certain plain and precious things about the process of prayer are left through the Holy Bible to assume that if they ask in faith, it will be granted: "For every one that asketh receiveth; and he that seeketh findeth; and to him that knocketh it shall be opened." (Matthew 7:8.) "And all things, whatsoever ye shall ask in prayer, believing, ye shall receive." (Matthew 21:22.)

For a more full understanding of prayer, these disclosing and refining verses are vital:

> Yea, I know that God will give liberally to him that asketh. Yea, my God will give me, if I ask not amiss... (2 Nephi 4:35.)

> And now, if God, who has created you, on whom you are dependent for your lives and for all that ye have and are, doth grant unto you whatsoever ye ask that is right, in faith, believing that ye shall receive, O then, how ye ought to impart of the substance that ye have one to another. (Mosiah 4:21.)

And whatsoever ye shall ask the Father in my name, which is right, believing that ye shall receive, behold it shall be given unto you. (3 Nephi 18:20.)

The matured disciple can be even further blessed by having his very petitions inspired. Then yet another and an awesome dimension of prayer unfolds:

And now, because thou hast done this with such unwearyingness, behold, I will bless thee forever; and I will make thee mighty in word and in deed, in faith and in works; yea, even that all things shall be done unto thee according to thy word, for thou shalt not ask that which is contrary to my will. (Helaman 10:5.)

He that asketh in the Spirit asketh according to the will of God; wherefore it is done even as he asketh. (D&C 46:30.)

These are not minor clarifications and amplifications. Sincere and good men and women—if they have not "stumbled"—at least have been perplexed because of their not having these plain and precious instructions and insights before them. Able and articulate souls have been left to wonder aloud over the Lord's seemingly unqualified promise. One such person was C. S. Lewis, about whom we read the following:

Lewis acknowledged that there is a problem in the New Testament about petitionary prayer. The promises seem explicit and unqualified. "Whatever you ask for in my name you will receive." True enough, the corrective is generally nearby: just as a human parent would not give a stone to a child who asked for bread, or a snake to a child who asked for a fish, so God will often not give us the stone we ask for thinking it to be bread—he gives us real bread instead. How many of us who have prayed fervently for something have been very glad in retrospect that we did not get it!

Still, a problem remains: not the problem of why God sometimes refuses us, but the problem of why the promises seem too unqualified: "...I have no answer to my problem, though I have taken it to about every Christian I know, learned or simple, lay or clerical, within my own Communion or without."

> Perhaps this is partly a problem created by applying in too general a fashion statements made by Christ to those in very special circumstances.[1]

Doctrinal clarifications contained in the "other books" of scripture are scarcely such as would come from a mere copyist. In fact, these additional scriptures lie at the very heart of understanding the vital doctrine of prayer, which comprises man's primary pattern of personal communication with God. How "plain and precious" these are! How fitting that we should be blessed with needed clarification concerning the vital and central doctrine of prayer, especially as we strive to communicate with the God of the glorious resurrection!

Another of the most significant "restorations," or amplifications of something "plain and precious," may be seen by juxtaposing the following verses from the Bible and modern revelation concerning status, the use of authority and power by those who are called to represent the Lord:

For many are called but few are chosen. (Matthew 22:14.)

For ye see your calling, brethren, how that not many wise men after the flesh, not many mighty, not many noble, are called. (1 Corinthians 1:26.)

Behold, there are many called, but few are chosen. And why are they not chosen?

Because their hearts are set so much upon the things of this world, and aspire to the honors of men, that they do not learn this one lesson—

That the rights of the priesthood are inseparably connected with the powers of heaven, and that the powers of heaven cannot be controlled nor handled only

upon the principles of
righteousness.

That they may be con-
ferred upon us, it is true; but
when we undertake to cover
our sins, or to gratify our
pride, our vain ambition, or
to exercise control or
dominion or compulsion
upon the souls of the
children of men, in any
degree of unrighteousness,
behold, the heavens with-
draw themselves; the Spirit
of the Lord is grieved; and
when it is withdrawn, Amen
to the priesthood or the
authority of that man. . . .

We have learned by sad
experience that it is the
nature and disposition of
almost all men, as soon as
they get a little authority, as
they suppose, they will im-
mediately begin to exercise
unrighteous dominion.

Hence many are called,
but few are chosen. (D&C
121:34-37, 39-40.)

Surely in the meridian of time Jesus gave more, at least to
His Twelve, than the intriguing and surviving statement in
Matthew. Only centuries later, however, did we receive the
needed "plain and precious" elaboration.

How much human suffering there has been, is, and still will be because of the usual worldly way of exercising power! Each of us has experienced, in one degree or another, the world's way. Compared with that way, we have now received the heavenly manner in which priesthood power should be exercised. And why not all forms of dominion and power? How many forgetful or unappreciative Pharaohs have come along who knew not the Josephs? (See Exodus 1:8; Acts 7:18.)

The insensitivities, the short memories, the transitions of mortal power, often ugly and violent, amply attest to the substance and style that so often accompany the misuse and play of mortal power. But the true Christian is told plainly that his style and substance must become different.

Indeed, in modern scriptures when the Lord describes the desired attributes (persuasion, long-suffering, gentleness, meekness, love unfeigned, kindness, and pure knowledge), are not these the very virtues of God Himself? the style and substance of His leadership? No wonder God desires His priesthood power to be used in those ways, for His power must be used in His way.

How vital, therefore, is the attribute of meekness! All the books of scripture unite in telling us it is so. Using the example of meekness, an undervalued virtue which is so often brushed aside in our day, we can see how the disregard of a gospel attribute can be a stumbling block to one's spiritual development.

Meekness is one of the attributes of Deity. It is significant to see how our understanding of the need for that attribute is enhanced by drawing upon *all* the scriptures, not just a few. Jesus, our Lord and Exemplar, called attention to Himself as being "meek and lowly in heart." (Matthew 11:29.) Paul extolled the "meekness and gentleness of Christ." (2 Corinthians 10:1.) The Greek rendition of the word *meek* in the New Testament, by the way, is "gentle and humble."

Actually, meekness is an attribute that is essential not

merely for itself. Moroni declared it is also vital because one cannot develop those other crucial virtues without meekness: "And the remission of sins bringeth meekness, and lowliness of heart; and because of meekness and lowliness of heart cometh the visitation of the Holy Ghost, which Comforter filleth with hope and perfect love, which love endureth by diligence unto prayer, until the end shall come, when all the saints shall dwell with God." (Moroni 8:26.)

In the ecology of the eternal attributes, these cardinal characteristics are inextricably bound up together. Among them, meekness is often the initiator, facilitator, and consolidator.

Moreover, if one needs further persuasion as to how vital this virtue is, Moroni warned that "none is acceptable before God, save the meek and the lowly in heart." (Moroni 7:44.) If we could but believe in the reality of that bold, but accurate, declaration, then you and I would find ourselves focusing on the crucial rather than the marginal traits. We would then cease pursuing lifestyles that, inevitably and irrevocably, are going out of style.

We live in coarsening times, times in which meekness is both misunderstood and despised. Yet it has been, is, and will remain a nonnegotiable dimension of true discipleship; its development is a remarkable achievement anytime, but especially in this age. Therefore, how needed are the many fresh, but plain, scriptural reminders of the necessity of the precious virtue of meekness!

Perhaps what we brought with us as intelligences into our creation as spirit children constitutes a given within which even God must work. Add to that possibility the certain reality of God's deep commitment to our free agency, and we begin to see how essential meekness is.

We need to learn so much. Yet we are free to choose. (See 2 Nephi 2:27.) How crucial it is to be teachable! Since there is no other way in which God could do what He is determined to do, no wonder He and His prophets emphasize meekness so often.

Since God desired to have us become like Himself, He first had to make us free to learn, to choose, and to experience. Our humility and teachability are premiere determinants of both our progress and our happiness. Agency is essential to perfect-ability, and meekness is essential to the wise use of agency and to our recovery when we've misused agency.

Let us not brush by this developmental premise. The scriptures are as one concerning life's premises and purposes; they make it clear that we are to become like the Father and His Son, Jesus Christ: "Be ye therefore perfect, even as your Father which is in heaven is perfect." (Matthew 5:48.) "Therefore I would that ye should be perfect even as I, or your Father who is in heaven is perfect." (3 Nephi 12:48.) "Therefore, what manner of men ought ye to be? Verily I say unto you, even as I am." (3 Nephi 27:27.) It is an awesome objective—impossible of attainment without meekness.

The Father and our Savior desire to lead us through love, for if we were merely driven where they wish us to go, we would not be worthy to be there, and surely we could not stay there. They are Shepherds, not sheepherders.

In that premortal council wherein Jesus meekly volunteered to aid the Father's plan, saying, "Here am I, send me" (Abraham 3:27), it was one of those special moments when a few words are preferred to many. Never has one individual offered, in so few words, to do so much for so many as did Jesus when He meekly proffered Himself as ransom for all of us—billions upon billions of us.

Moses was once described as being the most meek man on the face of the earth; yet we recall his impressive boldness in the courts of Pharaoh and his scalding indignation following his descent from Sinai. (Numbers 12:3.)

Meekness also cultivates in us a generosity in viewing the mistakes and imperfections of others. Moroni wrote, "Condemn me not because of mine imperfection, neither my father, because of his imperfection, . . . but rather give thanks unto God that he hath made manifest unto you our imperfections, that ye may learn to be more wise than we have been." (Mormon 9:31.)

For those of us who are too concerned about status or being last in line or losing our place, we need to read again those words about how the "last shall be first" and "the first shall be last." (Matthew 19:30.) Assertiveness is not automatically bad, of course, but if we fully understood the motives that underlie some of our acts of assertion, we would be embarrassed. Frankly, when others perceive such motivations, they are sometimes embarrassed for us.

Meekness does not mean tentativeness. Rather, it means thoughtfulness. Meekness makes room for others. "Let nothing be done through strife or vainglory; but in lowliness of mind let each esteem other better than themselves." (Philippians 2:3.)

We admire boldness and dash, but boldness and dash can so easily slip into pomp and panache. By contrast, the meek are able with regularity to peel off the encrustations of ego that form on one's soul like barnacles on a ship. The meek are thus able to avoid the abuse of authority and power—a tendency to which the Lord declared almost all succumb. (See D&C 121:39.) All, that is, except the meek!

The meek use power and authority properly, no doubt because their gentleness and meekness reflect a love unfeigned, a genuine caring. Their influence is "maintained . . . only by persuasion, by long-suffering, by gentleness and meekness, and by love unfeigned." (D&C 121:41.)

Meekness permits us to be confident, as Nephi declared, of that which we do know—even when we do not yet know the meaning of all other things. (See 1 Nephi 11:17.) Meekness constitutes a continuing invitation to continuing education. No wonder the Lord reveals His secrets to the meek, for they are "easy to be entreated." (Alma 7:23.) Being more teachable, the meek continuously receive, with special appreciation, what the apostle James called "the engrafted word." (James 1:21.) They receive, as Joseph Smith described it, the pure flow of intelligence—all from the divine databank.[2]

This mortal experience through which we are passing is one in which beauties, subtleties, and delicacies abound. Wonders lie all about us. The meek person who is observing will contemplate the lilies of the field, will ponder the galaxies, and will notice, and then lift up, those whose hands hang down. (D&C 81:5.)

Peter waxed poetic when he urged "the ornament of a meek and quiet spirit." (1 Peter 3:4.) A "meek and quiet spirit" is essential to our happiness here and hereafter, men and women alike. As with meekness, so it is with so many other plain and precious truths—the scriptures are symphonic in the music provided for the edification of the soul.

Another of the most significant contributions—including both clarification and elaboration—made by the revelations given to us in modern times has to do with God's omniscience and human freedom. This likewise is no small matter. Confusion concerning this interface has caused many to stumble or at least to hold back from full devotion. The seeming dilemma has been put perceptively and well in these words:

> Consider a problem that has bothered many believers: if God knows everything, then God knows the future. But if God knew yesterday what I will do tomorrow, how can I be free, as I believe I am, to do or not to do certain things tomorrow? ...
>
> Thus, two ideas basic to Christianity, God's omniscience on the one hand and human freedom and responsibility on the other, seem incompatible.[3]

But modern revelations make it abundantly clear that God is not "in time" in the manner that we mortals are. This is precisely what some able and perceptive commentators have surmised as they have wrestled sincerely with this dilemma, though without "plain and precious" modern scriptures. For example, the philosopher Boethius described in the fifth century how "God is outside of time and does not foresee the future; rather, he sees it in an 'eternal now' that is equally present to all parts of time. God did not know yesterday what I will do tomorrow; he sees timelessly in eternity 'what I am doing' in the future just as he sees what I am doing now. We must be careful not to conclude that since past, present, and future are equally present to God, they are equally present to each other. Both space and time are real, not just illusions, but God created them both and is not bound by either."[4] Besides, we mortals make our decisions within *our* framework of understanding, not God's.

The modern revelations give needed clarification and confirmation concerning God's omniscience through these significant insights when laid alongside those from the Bible:

His understanding is infinite. (Psalm 147:5.)

God . . . knoweth all things. (1 John 3:20.)

And hath made of one blood all nations of men for to dwell on all the face of the earth, and hath determined the times before appointed, and the bounds of their habitation. (Acts 17:26.)

O how great the holiness of our God! For he knoweth all things, and there is not anything save he knows it. (2 Nephi 9:20.)

The Lord knoweth all things from the beginning; wherefore, he prepareth a way to accomplish all his works among the children of men; for behold, he hath all power unto the fulfilling of all his words. And thus it is. Amen. (1 Nephi 9:6.)

In the presence of God
... all things for their glory
are manifest, past, present,
and future, and are contin-
ually before the Lord. (D&C
130:7. See also 88:41.)

All things are present
before mine eyes. (D&C
38:2.)

All things are present
with me, for I know them
all. (Moses 1:6.)

These verses confirm what has been referred to as "the eternal now"—within which God exists, so that He sees rather than foresees.

We mortals, of course, cannot and dare not boast of our own puny knowledge and wisdom. But we can, safely and justifiably, do as Alma did: "boasting in my God; for he has all power, all wisdom, and all understanding; he comprehendeth all things." (Alma 26:35.) And thus how much more we can fully trust God!

Furthermore, modern revelations in particular seem to suggest that there is a hierarchy of truth in which all facts are not of equal significance. Nephi and Paul, demonstrably united in their assertions, are likewise correlated in their teachings, including in the matter under discussion: "And now I, Nephi, cannot say more; the Spirit stoppeth mine utterance, and I am left to mourn because ... men ... will not search knowledge, nor understand great knowledge, when is it given unto them in plainness, even as plain as word can be." (2 Nephi 32:7.) "But God hath revealed them unto us by his Spirit: for the Spirit searcheth all things, yea, the deep things of God." (1 Corinthians 2:10.)

There is no democracy among truths. In fact, among those verities which matter most are those which can help us mortals, at least in some things, to draw upon truths that transcend time. For God, the past, the present, and the future are one. In fact, in modern scriptures the Lord has even defined truth as a time-spanning "knowledge of things as they are, and as they were, and as they are to come." (D&C 93:24.) Truth is, indeed, time-spanning, for "truth abideth and hath no end." (D&C 88:66.)

One ancient group was described as "highly favored" of the Lord. Why? Primarily because of economic blessings? No, because certain multidimensional and time-transcending facts were made known to them, "having been such a highly favored people of the Lord, . . . having had all things made known unto them, according to their desires, and their faith, and prayers, of that which has been, and which is, and which is to come." (Alma 9:20.) The truths given to those favored people provided a precious perspective, a longitudinality that time-bound, mortal man especially needs.

Just how crucial access is to time-transcending truth may be pondered in the setting in which Sherem, an agnostic, berated a prophet for preaching a Christ to come "many hundred years hence." Sherem declared that "there should be no Christ." Indeed, he said, it was even blasphemous for prophets to teach of things to come, for "no man knoweth of such things; for he cannot tell of things to come." (Jacob 7:1-7.) The anti-Christ was a "here and now" person who, ironically, put himself forward as if he were the judge of what constituted orthodoxy. So, alas, today—like Sherem, who ostensibly wished to uphold the law of Moses—some denounce modern prophets for telling of plain and precious things yet to come. Provincialism wears many blinders, and each is designed to deflect those fundamental truths which transcend time. How relentlessly the adversary seeks to grind mortals down to a single plane, knowing, as he does, that if mortals can be confined to now, then it is so easy to declare present appetite, instead of Jesus, as king.

One vital role of a seer is that he can so transcend time. Ammon in the Book of Mormon tells us that "a seer can know of things which are past, and also of things which are to come, and by them shall all things be revealed, or, rather, shall secret things be made manifest, and hidden things shall come to light, and things which are not known shall be made known by them, and also things shall be made known by them which otherwise could not be known." (Mosiah 8:17.)

Furthermore, the prophet Jacob in the Book of Mormon speaks about how the Spirit of our Heavenly Father will tell us the truth about "things as they really are, and of things as they really will be." (Jacob 4:13.)

These truths carry many implications that, even with the precious and helpful clarification, are too magnificent for mere mortals to manage fully. But they tell us enough to help us to trust even more deeply in the manner in which God balances our agency and His omniscience.

This pleading from King Benjamin shows the way to regard and adore our omniscient God: "Believe in God; believe that he is, and that he created all things, both in heaven and in earth; believe that he has all wisdom, and all power, both in heaven and in earth; believe that man doth not comprehend all the things which the Lord can comprehend." (Mosiah 4:9.)

As we are overwhelmed by the powerful truths God has given us in the scriptures, it becomes important for us, even if we are perplexed in the presence of these powerful truths, to remember the ultimate assurances. For now, these are the things we most need to know, the grand truths that can make us free. (See John 8:32.) We can be free at last from ignorance concerning our identity and life's purposes, and free from the heavy despair of mortal provincialism.

Nephi exemplified such bedrock trust in God and His purposes so well: "I know that [God] loveth his children; nevertheless, I do not know the meaning of all things." (1 Nephi 11:17.)

It is enough for us to believe that man does not comprehend all the things the Lord can comprehend, resting assured until that later moment when we will be better able to understand the magnificence of the truths He has generously and reassuringly bequeathed to us.

Meanwhile, these added truths surely do give us things that are truly "plain and precious." They also warn us about distinguishing between mere information and great knowledge, between postulates and wisdom, lest, as Paul said, we join the ranks of those mortals who are "ever learning, and never able to come to a knowledge of the truth." (2 Timothy 3:7.)

Furthermore, they make more clear the relationship of faith and knowledge. Faith is not devoid of intellectual content, nor is it antireason. Spiritual things belong to an encircling and larger realm. This realm has its own culture, its own evidence, its own interior consistency, and, indeed, its own language. Toward this realm, ironically, the "natural man" will not extend even a mild form of diplomatic recognition. Paul explained:

> But God hath revealed them unto us by his Spirit: for the Spirit searcheth all things, yea, the deep things of God.
>
> For what man knoweth the things of a man, save the spirit of man which is in him? even so the things of God knoweth no man, but the Spirit of God.
>
> Now we have received, not the spirit of the world, but the spirit which is of God; that we might know the things that are freely given to us of God.
>
> Which things also we speak, not in the words which man's wisdom teacheth, but which the Holy Ghost teacheth; comparing spiritual things with spiritual.
>
> But the natural man receiveth not the things of the Spirit of God: for they are foolishness unto him: neither can he know them, because they are spiritually discerned. (1 Corinthians 2:10-14.)

Secular scoffing cannot make this real and distinctive realm of the Spirit go away. How blessed we are to have so many new spiritual truths given to us—especially in an era in which so many doubt or deny the existence of absolute truths!

It is essential for us to have an unobstructed view of the strait and narrow path. The consummate challenge of taking up the cross daily is demanding enough without our being vexed by stumbling blocks, a lack of direction, or a lack of clarity concerning the purposes of life.

Notes

1. Richard L. Purtill, *C. S. Lewis's Case for the Christian Faith* (San Francisco: Harper & Row, 1981), p. 113.
2. "The Spirit of Revelation is in connection with these blessings. A person may profit by noticing the first intimation of the spirit of revelation; for instance, when you feel pure intelligence flowing into you, it may give you sudden strokes of ideas, so that by noticing it, you may find it fulfilled the same day or soon; (i.e.) those things that were presented unto your minds by the Spirit of God, will come to pass; and thus by learning the Spirit of God and understanding it, you may grow into the principle of revelation, until you become perfect in Christ Jesus." (Joseph Smith, *History of the Church* 3:381.)
3. Purtill, *op. cit.*, p. 30.
4. Ibid., p. 31.

Chapter 6
Taking Up the Cross Daily

If one is in search of reassuring gospel ground rules pertaining to life with its challenge of carrying the cross daily (Luke 9:23), are not the following companion verses given to us by Nephi and Paul, respectively, truly essential?

> And it came to pass that I, Nephi, said unto my father: I will go and do the things which the Lord hath commanded, for I know that the Lord giveth no commandments unto the children of men, save he shall prepare a way for them that they may accomplish the thing which he commandeth them. (1 Nephi 3:7.)

> There hath no temptation taken you but such as is common to man: but God is faithful, who will not suffer you to be tempted above that ye are able; but will with the temptation also make a way to escape, that ye may be able to bear it. (1 Corinthians 10:13.)

Again, we see the correlation of prophets concerning certain ground rules in life with regard to meeting either challenge or temptation.

As evidenced so many times, the conceptual consistency and the lack of doctrinal deviance are their own witnesses to the divine authorship of the various books of scripture. Observe how fundamental this declaration is: "For behold, the Spirit of Christ is given to every man, that he may know good from evil." (Moroni 7:16.) This constitutes another of those fundamental ground rules to aid our understanding about human accountability. Notice how the scripture is buttressed by these quotations from yet another of the "other books" of scripture: "And the Spirit giveth light to every man that cometh into the world; and the Spirit enlighteneth every man through the world, that hearkeneth to the voice of the Spirit." (D&C 84:46.) "And that I am the true light that lighteth every man that cometh into the world." (D&C 93:2.)

Not only are these declarations consistent with each other, but they also constitute, once again, an amplification of the inspired New Testament assertions by one of the original Twelve Apostles of the Lamb: "That was the true Light, which lighteth every man that cometh into the world." (John 1:9.)

Just how much light that human being has who lives in a primitive tribe in some remote jungle, we do not know precisely. Nor, indeed, are we given the full understanding as to whether or not that light can be fully extinguished by egregious sin. But these strong strands of doctrine are clearly intertwined.

Likewise, should we not purposefully pair insightful and reassuring scriptures such as the following, which are as central as they are simple: "Adam fell that men might be; and men are, that they might have joy." (2 Nephi 2:25.) "For as in Adam all die, even so in Christ shall all be made alive." (1 Corinthians 15:22.)

Not only do we see conceptual consistency throughout the many books of scripture, but we also see clearly examples of certain precious principles in action. Contemplating such case studies can help us as we disciples strive to do what Jesus said we must—take up the cross daily.

Many of us have been deeply touched by the episode involving Martha and Mary in which Jesus instructs us all. In their choices between the duties of the day (the things of the moment) and the things of eternal value, Mary chose "that good part which shall not be taken away from her." (Luke 10:42.) No wonder we can rejoice in reading with enhanced understanding those same touching words as Lehi prepared to depart the mortal scene: "I have spoken these few words unto you all, my sons, in the last days of my probation; and I have chosen the good part, according to the words of the prophet. And I have none other object save it be the everlasting welfare of your souls." (2 Nephi 2:30.)

Surely Lehi had "chosen the good part." Surely, as the Lord's prophets align themselves with God's purposes, we should not be surprised to see Lehi's motivations focused on "the everlasting welfare of your souls." Lehi was the servant of God, who does nothing "save it be for the benefit of the world." (2 Nephi 26:24.)

Having been intrigued by the following verse in Luke, we should ponder the implications of being an "unprofitable servant": "So likewise ye, when ye shall have done all those things which are commanded you, say, We are unprofitable servants: we have done that which was our duty to do." (Luke 17:10.) But the pondering will be more productive if we include in our ponderings the truly marvelous amplification in the Book of Mormon:

> I say unto you that if ye should serve him who has created you from the beginning, and is preserving you from day to day, by lending you breath, that ye may live and move and do according to your own will, and even supporting you from one moment to another—I say, if ye should serve him with all your whole souls yet ye would be unprofitable servants.
>
> And behold, all that he requires of you is to keep his commandments; and he has promised you that if ye would keep his commandments ye should prosper in the land; and he never doth vary from that which he hath said; therefore, if ye do keep his commandments he doth bless you and prosper you.
>
> And now, in the first place, he hath created you, and granted unto you your lives, for which ye are indebted unto him.
>
> And secondly, he doth require that ye should do as he hath commanded you; for which if ye do, he doth immediately bless you; and therefore he hath paid you. And ye are still indebted unto him, and

are, and will be, forever and ever; therefore, of what have ye to boast? And now I ask, can ye say aught of yourselves? I answer you, Nay. Ye cannot say that ye are even as much as the dust of the earth; yet ye were created of the dust of the earth; but behold, it belongeth to him who created you. (Mosiah 2:21-25.)

To those who have been captured by the spirit of self-sufficiency that so often goes with secular things, these verses are particularly important for engendering humility in our daily living.

Illustrative of the further tactical counsel we receive for daily living, which is far more than incidental, are the following verses, preserved especially for the special benefit of the truly conscientious who should learn to pace themselves in wisdom:

> And see that all these things are done in wisdom and order; for it is not requisite that a man should run faster than he has strength. And again, it is expedient that he should be diligent, that thereby he might win the prize; therefore, all things must be done in order. (Mosiah 4:27.)

> Do not run faster or labor more than you have strength and means provided to enable you to translate; but be diligent unto the end. (D&C 10:4.)

> And the apostles gathered themselves together unto Jesus, and told him all things, both what they had done, and what they had taught. And he said unto them, Come ye yourselves apart into a desert place, and rest a while: for there were many coming and going, and they had no leisure so much as to eat. And they departed into a desert place by ship privately. (Mark 6:30-32.)

Will we ever receive a more demanding test of our personal philanthropy than the unconditional and nonjudgmental standard raised up in the following verses from Mosiah?

> And also, ye yourselves will succor those that stand in need of your succor; ye will administer of your substance unto him that standeth in need; and ye will not suffer that the beggar putteth up his petition to you in vain, and turn him out to perish.

Perhaps thou shalt say: The man has brought upon himself his misery; therefore I will stay my hand, and will not give unto him of my food, nor impart unto him of my substance that he may not suffer, for his punishments are just —

But I say unto you, O man, whosoever doeth this the same hath great cause to repent; and except he repenteth of that which he hath done he perisheth forever, and hath no interest in the kingdom of God. (Mosiah 4:16-18.)

The Book of Mormon gives us an excellent chance to compare the skepticism, disbelief, and pride of our time with that which prevailed in circumstances centuries ago:

Therefore, as Aaron entered into one of their synagogues to preach unto the people, and as he was speaking unto them, behold there arose an Amalekite and began to contend with him, saying: What is that thou hast testified? Hast thou seen an angel? Why do not angels appear unto us? Behold are not this people as good as thy people? (Alma 21:5.)

We also see rationalization in the raw:

And they began to reason and to contend among themselves, saying: That it is not reasonable that such a being as a Christ shall come; if so, and he be the Son of God, the Father of heaven and of earth, as it has been spoken, why will he not show himself unto us as well as unto them who shall be at Jerusalem? (Helaman 16:18.)

Likewise open to plain view are the consequences of lapsed faith:

And thus we can plainly discern, that after a people have been once enlightened by the Spirit of God, and have had great knowledge of things pertaining to righteousness, and then have fallen away into sin and transgression, they become more hardened, and thus their state becomes worse than though they had never known these things. (Alma 24:30.)

We see variations in disbelievers, such as the paradox of some who believe vaguely but whose beliefs are not connected with their daily behavior. Some assume that the god they worship is a very permissive as well as passive god.

Empty homage to a passive deity inevitably results in a permissive laity, as Alma explains: "Now this was the tradition of Lamoni, which he had received from his father, that there was a Great Spirit. Notwithstanding they believed in a Great Spirit, they supposed that whatsoever they did was right." (Alma 18:5.)

We can better understand, therefore, why the adversary is anxious that people not be given those particularized saving truths that pertain to the past, present, and future. In the Book of Mormon we see several incidents of people who strayed and faltered because of their proud provincialism, and who then stoutly maintained that they could not know that which is to come. One example is the Zoramites, who, Alma said, "did offer up, every man, the self-same prayer unto God, thanking their God that they were chosen of him, and that he did not lead them away after the tradition of their brethren, and that their hearts were not stolen away to believe in things to come, which they knew nothing about." (Alma 31:22.)

How fascinating to see adherence to a false religion in which superficial ritual, proud contentment, and a haughty rejection of prophecy were so adroitly combined! Sanctioned agnosticism can be very insistent on its own orthodoxy.

The precious perspective that the gospel gives us and that is a part of the faith we need to develop is bound up in the plan of salvation. This perspective, which the adversary so strongly resists our having, is precisely the one-dimensional view of life that clearly undergirds so much of agnosticism, whether ancient or modern. Hearts that are stolen away from eternal perspectives inevitably become fixed and set upon the immediate and upon the things of this world. Time-transcending truths that tell mortals who they are and why they are here are the very truths the adversary most resists and fears. Hence his scoffing is so severe when things messianic are mixed with a foretelling of the future.

For instance, refusing to acknowledge not only the existence of God but also His role as a tutoring Father is what makes becoming a loving brother difficult. Moreover, when proud self-sufficiency is a credo of conduct, ethical relativism is not far behind. Korihor, the anti-Christ, is an example of this. He told the people that "there could be no atonement made for the sins of men, but every man fared in this life according to the management of the creature; therefore every man prospered according to his genius, and that every man conquered according to this strength; and whatsoever a man did was no crime." (Alma 30:17.)

Moreover, those lacking religious commitment sometimes resent it in others. Moroni said to the wicked Zerahemnah, "Behold, we have not come out to battle against you that we might shed your blood for power; neither do we desire to bring any one to the yoke of bondage. But this is the very cause for which ye have come against us; yea, and ye are angry with us because of our religion." (Alma 44:2.)

Understandably, therefore, the Book of Mormon would be of special importance inasmuch as it was to spread forth in an age with striking similarities to our own when "there shall be great pollutions upon the face of the earth; there shall be murders, and robbing, and lying, and deceivings, and whoredoms, and all manner of abominations; when there shall be many who will say, Do this, or do that, and it mattereth not, for the Lord will uphold such at the last day. But wo unto such for they are in the gall of bitterness and in the bonds of iniquity." (Mormon 8:31.)

How can behavioral standards matter much in the minds of those—then or now—who hold such an undemanding view of salvation? Nehor, a Nephite apostate, "testified unto the people that all mankind should be saved at the last day, and that they need not fear nor tremble, but that they might lift up their heads and rejoice; for the Lord had created all men, and had also redeemed all men; and, in the end, all men should have eternal life." (Alma 1:4.)

Such democratic deviousness!

Clever but pathetic Korihor surely has his modern counterparts, especially in today's settings in which so many people are especially free to choose for themselves. In his time (as in ours), "there was no law against a man's belief; for it was strictly contrary to the commands of God that there should be a law which should bring men on to unequal grounds. For thus saith the scripture: Choose ye this day, whom ye will serve. Now if a man desired to serve God, it was his privilege; or rather, if he believed in God it was his privilege to serve him; but if he did not believe in him there was no law to punish him." (Alma 30:7-9.)

Soon we may see such situations in which there will be "no laws against a man's belief," but also few laws against a man's behavior. As Korihor contended so articulately and agnostically, "O ye that are bound down under a foolish and a vain hope, why do ye yoke yourselves with such foolish things? Why do ye look for a Christ? For no man can know of anything which is to come. . . . How do ye know of their surety? Behold, ye cannot know of things which ye do not see; therefore ye cannot know that there shall be a Christ." (Alma 30:13, 15.)

In the denouncement of Korihor to follow, discerning Alma said: "Behold, I know that thou believest, but thou art possessed with a lying spirit, and ye have put off the Spirit of God that it may have no place in you; but the devil has power over you, and he doth carry you about, working devices that he may destroy the children of God." (Alma 30:41-42.)

Then Korihor confessed: "But behold, the devil hath deceived me; for he appeared unto me in the form of an angel, and said unto me: Go and reclaim this people, for they have all gone astray after an unknown God. And he said unto me: There is no God; yea, and he taught me that which I should say. And I have taught his words; and I taught them because they were pleasing unto the carnal mind; and I taught them, even until I had much success, insomuch that I verily believed that they were true; and for this cause I withstood the truth, even until I have brought this great curse upon me." (Alma 30:53.)

At first reading, this episode may seem too simplistic. But the brevity of the report does not argue against its validity. It contains several elements that are fascinating even though they were not further developed. There was the zeal to shake the faith of believers. (How often has intolerance covered itself in the cloak of pluralism?) There was the almost inevitable responsiveness of those misled, because Korihor's message was "pleasing to the carnal mind," with all that that implies; success and self-deception were intertwined. And there was adroit use of political and religious freedom.

King Agrippa withstood the truth with his mind when his heart told him otherwise, as Paul found when he described his own former persecution of the Saints:

> For the king knoweth of these things, before whom also I speak freely: for I am persuaded that none of these things are hidden from him; for this thing was not done in a corner.
> King Agrippa, believest thou the prophets? I know that thou believest.
> Then Agrippa said unto Paul, Almost thou persuadest me to be a Christian. (Acts 26:26-28.)

Agrippa has his counterparts in our own time. And then as now, those less vested in the establishment of the world, or scorned by it, often responded with alacrity to the gospel message: "And the common people heard him gladly." (Mark 12:37.) "And he lifted up his eyes on his disciples, and said,

"Blessed be ye poor: for yours is the kingdom of God." (Luke 6:20.) "Then Jesus answering said unto them, Go your way, and tell John what things ye have seen and heard; how that . . . to the poor the gospel is preached." (Luke 7:20.)

This was true also of those whom Alma taught: "And it came to pass that after much labor among them, they began to have success among the poor class of people; for behold, they were cast out of the synagogues because of the coarseness of their apparel." (Alma 32:2.)

We see subtleties even in the relationships of the generations. Eli of old had grave difficulty with the rising generation of his own household, for "his sons made themselves vile, and he restrained them not." (1 Samuel 3:13.)

To the Eli episode we can add these illustrative verses: "And also all that generation were gathered unto their fathers: and there arose another generation after them, which knew not the Lord, nor yet the works which he had done for Israel." (Judges 2:10.) "Now they did not sin ignorantly, for they knew the will of God concerning them, for it had been taught unto them; therefore they did wilfully rebel against God." (3 Nephi 6:18.)

The rising generation can, ironically, prove influentially interactive with the older, especially if the latter is soft and undetermined: "And there was also a cause of much sorrow among the Lamanites; for behold, they had many children who did grow up and began to wax strong in years, that they became for themselves, and were led away by some who were Zoramites, by their lyings and their flattering words, to join those Gadianton robbers. And thus were the Lamanites afflicted also, and began to decrease as to their faith and righteousness, because of the wickedness of the rising generation." (3 Nephi 1:29-30.)

The decade of the 1960s in America was one in which too many adults, insecure and uncertain, not only gave way to the

permissive pressures of some in the "rising generation" but then
actually adopted the lower lifestyle so promoted.

Willful dissent ages ago produced yet other symptoms that
are worthy of our pondering today as life confronts us with
determined dissenters who leave the Church—but who then
cannot leave the Church alone:

> Now these dissenters, having the same instruction and the same
> information of the Nephites, yea, having been instructed in the same
> knowledge of the Lord, nevertheless, it is strange to relate, not long
> after their dissensions they became more hardened and impenitent, and
> more wild, wicked and ferocious than the Lamanites—drinking in with
> the traditions of the Lamanites; giving way to indolence, and all manner
> of lasciviousness; yea, entirely forgetting the Lord their God. (Alma
> 47:36.)

Seldom does one encounter, especially so succinctly, the
awful manner in which hatred can be instilled, generation after
generation, in a whole people who were conditioned to feel
they had been wronged again and again:

> They were a wild, and ferocious, and a blood-thirsty people,
> believing in the tradition of their fathers, which is this—Believing that
> they were driven out of the land of Jerusalem because of the iniquities of
> their fathers, and that they were wronged in the wilderness by their
> brethren, and they were also wronged while crossing the sea;
> And again, that they were wronged while in the land of their first
> inheritance, after they had crossed the sea, and all this because that
> Nephi was more faithful in keeping the commandments of the
> Lord—therefore he was favored of the Lord, for the Lord heard his
> prayers and answered them, and he took the lead of their journey in the
> wilderness. (Mosiah 10:12-13.)

The result of this sad circumstance reflects not only
historical hostility, but "eternal hatred" as well: "And thus they
have taught their children that they should hate them, and that
they should murder them, and that they should rob and
plunder them, and do all they could to destroy them; therefore

they have an eternal hatred towards the children of Nephi." (Mosiah 10:17.)

Today's world trembles because of ancient grievances and hatreds, now nourished anew amid growing nuclear capacity. Surely such insights as the foregoing constitute sobering instruction!

The gradations of grief are set forth in the "other books" of scripture, such as those who found themselves in an awful and terrible psychological no-man's-land: "But behold this my joy was vain, for their sorrowing was not unto repentance, because of the goodness of God; but it was rather the sorrowing of the damned, because the Lord would not always suffer them to take happiness in sin. And they did not come unto Jesus with broken hearts and contrite spirits, but they did curse God, and wish to die. Nevertheless they would struggle with the sword for their lives." (Mormon 2:13-14.)

The positive counterpoint is there, too, such as with regard to how the testimony of one person can be interactively helpful to another. We read these declarative verses: "To some it is given by the Holy Ghost to know that Jesus Christ is the Son of God, and that he was crucified for the sins of the world. To others it is given to believe on their words, that they also might have eternal life if they continue faithful." (D&C 46:13-14.)

An instructive example of this principle in action is the relationship of Nephi to his brother Sam: "And I spake unto Sam, making known unto him the things which the Lord had manifested unto me by his Holy Spirit. And it came to pass that he believed in my words." (1 Nephi 2:17.) What a precious and practical insight to guide us in the relationships among neighbors and fellow citizens of the kingdom of God! Yet, as Lemuel demonstrated, interactiveness works the other way, too. (See 1 Nephi 3:28.)

Past circumstances can reassure us that others also have experienced that condition about which we sing as "our foes have rejoiced when our sorrows they've seen." (*Hymns,* no. 195.) We are given, for example, this perspective-yielding verse about the perversity of scoffers:

> And now it came to pass that I, Nephi, was exceedingly sorrowful because of the hardness of their hearts; and now when they saw that I began to be sorrowful they were glad in their hearts, insomuch that they did rejoice over me, saying: We knew that ye could not construct a ship, for we knew that ye were lacking in judgment; wherefore, thou canst not accomplish so great a work. (1 Nephi 17:19.)

As we strive to carry the cross daily, it is helpful to read how, though conditions change from century to century, the everlasting principles of the gospel stay constant, as we see in these interactive verses from Ether and Alma:

> And now as I said concerning faith—faith is not to have a perfect knowledge of things; therefore if ye have faith ye hope for things which are not seen, which are true. (Alma 32:21.)

> And now, behold, is your knowledge perfect? Yea, your knowledge is perfect in that thing, and your faith is dormant; and this because ye know. (Alma 32:34.)

> And because of the knowledge of this man he could not be kept from beholding within the veil; and he saw the finger of Jesus, which, when he saw, he fell with fear; for he knew that it was the finger of the Lord; and he had faith no longer, for he knew, nothing doubting. (Ether 3:19.)

The acquisition of personal spiritual knowledge, which is so vital, was well described by Paul:

> For after that in the wisdom of God the world by wisdom knew not God, it pleased God by the foolishness of preaching to save them that believe. (1 Corinthians 1:21.)

> For what man knoweth the things of a man, save the spirit of man which is in him? even so the things of God knoweth no man, but the Spirit of God. . . .

But the natural man receiveth not the things of the Spirit of God: for they are foolishness unto him: neither can he know them, because they are spiritually discerned. (1 Corinthians 2:11, 14.)

This very special process is further clarified by the Book of Mormon and the "other books" of scripture:

And I would not that ye think that I know of myself—not of the temporal but of the spiritual, not of the carnal mind but of God.

Now, behold, I say unto you, if I had not been born of God I should not have known these things. (Alma 36:4-5.)

And this is not all. Do ye not suppose that I know of these things myself? Behold, I testify unto you that I do know that these things whereof I have spoken are true. And how do ye suppose that I know of their surety?

Behold, I say unto you they are made known unto me by the Holy Spirit of God. Behold, I have fasted and prayed many days that I might know these things of myself. And now I do know of myself that they are true; for the Lord God hath made them manifest unto me by his Holy Spirit; and this is the spirit of revelation which is in me. (Alma 5:45-46.)

Not only is the realm of the spiritual real, but it is also filled with that which is knowable; however, this is only on the terms and in the process set forth by its Lord and Master.

The pairings and tandem expressions of truth are many indeed; illustrations abound that can do much to help us "take up the cross daily," such as the following:

And now Jared became exceedingly sorrowful because of the loss of the kingdom, for he had set his heart upon the kingdom and upon the glory of the world. (Ether 8:7.)

Because their hearts are set so much upon the things of this world, and aspire to the honors of men, that they do not learn this one lesson. (D&C 121:35.)

Nevertheless among the chief rulers also many believed on him; but because of the Pharisees they did not confess him, lest they should be put out of the synagogue: For they loved the praise of men more than the praise of God. (John 12:42-43.)

Nor are the blessed outcomes in daily behavior—which should occur as a result of keeping the commandments of God—neglected in the least in these "other books" of scripture. King Benjamin's sermon in chapter 4 of Mosiah is surely one of the greatest such sermons ever given:

> And behold, I say unto you that if ye do this ye shall always rejoice, and be filled with the love of God, and always retain a remission of your sins; and ye shall grow in the knowledge of the glory of him that created you, or in the knowledge of that which is just and true.
>
> And ye will not have a mind to injure one another, but to live peaceably, and to render to every man according to that which is his due.
>
> And ye will not suffer your children that they go hungry, or naked; neither will ye suffer that they transgress the laws of God, and fight and quarrel one with another, and serve the devil, who is the master of sin, or who is the evil spirit which hath been spoken of by our fathers, he being an enemy to all righteousness.
>
> But ye will teach them to walk in the ways of truth and soberness; ye will teach them to love one another, and to serve one another.
>
> And also, ye yourselves will succor those that stand in need of your succor; ye will administer of your substance unto him that standeth in need; and ye will not suffer that the beggar putteth up his petition to you in vain, and turn him out to perish. (Mosiah 4:12-16.)

Moreover, those who truly and worthily accept the baptismal covenant are already much-prepared to live in the special brotherhood and sisterhood described above. Alma taught:

> And now, as ye are desirous to come into the fold of God, and to be called his people, and are willing to bear one another's burdens, that they may be light; yea, and are willing to mourn with those that mourn; yea, and comfort those that stand in need of comfort, and to stand as witnesses of God at all times and in all things, and in all places that ye may be in, even until death, that ye may be redeemed of God, and be

numbered with those of the first resurrection, that ye may have eternal life. (Mosiah 18:8-9.)

Observe in the following the word portrait of how a whole people reflected such discipleship in their daily behavior:

> And they were among the people of Nephi, and also numbered among the people who were of the church of God. And they were also distinguished for their zeal towards God, and also towards men; for they were perfectly honest and upright in all things; and they were firm in the faith of Christ, even unto the end. (Alma 27:27.)

Where else but in the Book of Mormon do we get such an eloquent differentiation between that enforced humility which comes into being because of compelling circumstances and the true, intrinsic humility that occurs because of the word?

> I say unto you, it is well that ye are cast out of your synagogues, that ye may be humble, and that ye may learn wisdom; for it is necessary that ye should learn wisdom; for it is because that ye are cast out, that ye are despised of your brethren because of your exceeding poverty, that ye are brought to a lowliness of heart; for ye are necessarily brought to be humble.
>
> And now, because ye are compelled to be humble blessed are ye; for a man sometimes, if he is compelled to be humble, seeketh repentance; and now surely, whosoever repenteth shall find mercy; and he that findeth mercy and endureth to the end the same shall be saved.
>
> And now, as I said unto you, that because ye were compelled to be humble ye were blessed, do ye not suppose that they are more blessed who truly humble themselves because of the word? . . .
>
> For I do not mean that ye all of you have been compelled to humble yourselves; for I verily believe that there are some among you who would humble themselves, let them be in whatsoever circumstances they might. (Alma 32:12-14, 25.)

The terms upon which human happiness is obtainable are likewise clearly set forth, for in our use of free agency there must be rejection of wrong as well as acceptance of right:

> But behold, your days of probation are past; ye have procrastinated the day of your salvation until it is everlastingly too late, and your destruction is made sure; yea, for ye have sought all the days of your lives for that which ye could not obtain; and ye have sought for happiness in doing iniquity, which thing is contrary to the nature of that righteousness which is in our great and Eternal Head. (Helaman 13:38.)

> And now remember, remember, my brethren, that whosoever perisheth, perisheth unto himself; and whosoever doeth iniquity, doeth it unto himself; for behold, ye are free; ye are permitted to act for yourselves; for behold, God hath given unto you a knowledge and he hath made you free. (Helaman 14:30.)

The next reference is a superb example of the blending of inspiration and concision—a historical truth laid bare as a lesson for mankind: "Behold, I say unto you, wickedness never was happiness." (Alma 41:10.)

Yet it is not solely in amplification and clarification of things past that these other books of scripture are vitally helpful. They are essential to a better understanding of those things future that will surely have impact on our daily lives, depending upon the length of our mortal tenure.

The high utility of modern scriptures is especially evident in elaborating and clarifying that which is to come, the very dimension of knowledge that the adversary so consistently seeks to demean. Thus we can better prepare for and understand the modern events associated with the winding-up scenes—both grim and glorious—preceding the second coming of the Savior.

In seeking to analyze just what the scriptures tell those of us who live in a nuclear age regarding the destruction of the earth by fire and some of the related events in the last days, the author has found an interesting distribution of specific scriptural declarations. Of the nearly fifty scriptures used, five are from the Old Testament, three from the New Testament, twelve from the Book of Mormon, twenty from the Doctrine and Covenants, and two from the Pearl of Great Price. While not exhaustive, this is certainly indicative!

Actually, it should not surprise us that, for his people of the last days, the Lord would give such needed clarification and amplification. Moreover, the "other books" provide not only *more* data but also *crucial* data needed for any real understanding of both the promises and the problems associated with the coming cataclysms.

So it is that, in addition to the marvelous confirmation of Christ—His atonement, His resurrection, and His Lordship—these are splendid elaborations and clarifications of fundamental and basic doctrines with important guidelines for our daily lives.

There is yet another contribution made by the Book of Mormon—a further evidence of its divinity provided in a much more subtle way. In the examples of assorted gems to follow, there is as much poignancy as variety, as much to lift our standards as our hopes, as much to touch our hearts as to touch our minds!

Chapter 7

Assorted Gems in the "Other Books"

The variety of the assorted gems to be found in "these last records" is matched by their beauty. Yet what we find are more than apostolic aphorisms: these are truths that further deepen our trust in the unfolding purposes of our Father in heaven for the people on this planet and that show us God's careful preparations.

For example, in the Joseph Smith Translation, as Professor Matthews has observed, we learn more of Jesus' forty days in the wilderness:

> The KJV records that after his baptism Jesus was led by the Spirit into the wilderness "to be tempted of the devil. And when he had fasted forty days and forty nights, he was afterward an hungred." (Matt. 4:1-2.)
>
> The JST gives a different view:
>
> "Then Jesus was led up of the Spirit into the wilderness, *to be with God.*
>
> "And when he had fasted forty days and forty nights, *and had communed with God,* he was afterwards an hungered, *and was left to be tempted of the devil.*" (JST Matt. 4:1-2.)
>
> Furthermore, the account given by Luke states that Jesus was "forty days tempted of the devil." (Luke 4:2.) The JST alters this by saying, *"And after forty days, the devil came unto him, to tempt him."* (JST Luke 4:2.)
>
> The KJV further states in both Matthew and Luke that "the devil taketh" Jesus to a high mountain and also to a "pinnacle of the temple." However, according to the JST, it was not the devil but "the Spirit" who transported Jesus to these places, after which the devil then appeared to

him. (Compare KJV Matt. 4:5-8 and Luke 4:5-9 with JST Matt. 4:5-8 and Luke 4:5-9.)[1]

We likewise learn more about an important episode involving Jesus and little children:

> While in Galilee, Jesus placed a little child before his disciples and explained that the meekness and humility of little children are necessary qualifications for heaven. He emphasized children's favored status by declaring "that in heaven their angels do always behold the face of my Father which is in heaven. For the Son of man is come to save that which was lost." (KJV Matt. 18:10-11.)
>
> In the JST, Jesus enlarges upon this event: "For the Son of Man is come to save that which was lost, *and to call sinners to repentance; but these little ones have no need of repentance, and I will save them.*" (JST Matt. 18:11.)
>
> This single improvement is by itself significant, but it is followed by yet another event having to do with children. Following this episode in Galilee, Jesus traveled with his disciples into Judea some sixty miles to the south. While in Judea, there were "brought unto him little children, that he should put his hands on them, and pray: and the disciples rebuked them." (KJV Matt. 19:13.)
>
> Why the disciples acted as they did is not stated in the KJV, and the reader is left to wonder at their motives. Did they think Jesus was too busy? Or were they themselves annoyed by the interruption?
>
> Fortunately, the JST adds these clarifying words: ". . . And the disciples rebuked them, *saying, There is no need, for Jesus hath said, Such shall be saved.*" (JST Matt. 19:13.) From the text of the JST we see that the action of the disciples in Judea was influenced by the Savior's earlier teachings in Galilee. The JST clarifies the motives of the disciples, and speaks of the Savior's atoning sacrifice for little children. The reader's enjoyment of these two events is thereby significantly increased.[2]

Great and remarkable was Joseph, son of Jacob, a virtual prime minister of ancient Egypt and temporal savior of many in a time of ancient famine. One genuinely hungers to learn more than is contained in the Old Testament about this remarkable Joseph.

What do we learn of him in the pages of the Book of Mormon? In the case of Joseph's many-colored coat, the Old Testament tells us this: "Now Israel loved Joseph more than all his children, because he was the son of his old age: and he made him a coat of many colours." (Genesis 37:3.) "And the one went out from me, and I said, Surely he is torn in pieces; and I saw him not since." (Genesis 44:28.)

The Book of Mormon gives us a prophecy of Jacob that we do not find in Genesis:

> Moroni said unto them: Behold, we are a remnant of the seed of Jacob; yea, we are a remnant of the seed of Joseph, whose coat was rent by his brethren into many pieces; yea, and now behold, let us remember to keep the commandments of God, or our garments shall be rent by our brethren, and we be cast into prison, or be sold, or be slain.
>
> Yea, let us preserve our liberty as a remnant of Joseph; yea, let us remember the words of Jacob, before his death, for behold, he saw that a part of the remnant of the coat of Joseph was preserved and had not decayed. And he said—Even as this remnant of garment of my son hath been preserved, so shall a remnant of the seed of my son be preserved by the hand of God, and be taken unto himself, while the remainder of the seed of Joseph shall perish, even as the remnant of his garment. (Alma 46:23-24.)

We likewise learn that prescient Joseph saw not only the coming famine in Egypt, but he also "truly saw our day." (2 Nephi 3:5.) Twice he exclaimed joyfully over the promise given to him that the Lord would raise up a seer out of his seed. (2 Nephi 3:16-18.) In fact, the many prophecies of Joseph in Egypt (which we have yet to receive) are characterized thus: "For behold, he truly prophesied concerning all his seed. And the prophecies which he wrote, there are not many greater. And he prophesied concerning us, and our future generations; and they are written upon the plates of brass." (2 Nephi 4:2.)

Amid what must have been the loneliness of power attendant to Joseph's prestigious place as a Jew in Egyptian society and his many years away from his family, the added insights we receive concerning him are not surprising. The Old Testament tells us touchingly of Joseph's forgiving and generous nature toward his brothers who betrayed him; he found opportunity within what, in his earlier life, seemed to be tragedy:

> And he wept aloud: and the Egyptians and the house of Pharaoh heard.
> And Joseph said unto his brethren, I am Joseph; doth my father yet live? And his brethren could not answer him; for they were troubled at his presence.
> And Joseph said unto his brethren, Come near to me, I pray you. And they came near. And he said, I am Joseph your brother, whom ye sold into Egypt.
> Now therefore be not grieved, nor angry with yourselves, that ye sold me hither; for God did send me before you to preserve life. (Genesis 45:2-5.)

But surely Joseph, sophisticated in Egyptian politics, knew that a pharaoh would soon come who knew not Joseph nor his posterity. What, therefore, was the future of his seed? How understandable that Joseph would care so deeply about his posterity! No wonder he exclaimed over God's promise that a seer like Moses would be raised up from his seed in the last days to serve his seed. (See 2 Nephi 3:6-7.) And upon being told, as an indication of divine loyalty, that this seer would even bear his name, Joseph rejoiced. (See JST, Genesis 50:24-38.)

Just as the Holy Bible does not give us the full words uttered by Joseph in Egypt, it also does not contain at least one significant vision experienced by Moses—an experience that is found in one of the other books of scripture.

As recorded in Moses 1, this scene unfolded as Moses was caught up into an exceedingly high mountain and saw God face to face and talked with Him. At the end of that marvelous theophany, Moses was filled with overwhelming but precious perspective concerning the expansiveness of God's work. "Of this thing Moses bore record; but because of wickedness, it is not had among the children of men." (Moses 1:23.)

Again, one should reflect carefully upon "plain and precious things" given through Moses on this occasion that were not previously had "among the children of men." Among them were these: Moses saw the workmanship of God's hands, but not all. He was told that God's works are "without end." (A complete disclosure of God's works to man would mean that such a person could not "afterwards remain in the flesh on the earth.") God spoke to Moses of His omniscience: "All things are present with me, for I know them all."

Moses was so overwhelmed by the panorama he saw pertaining to this planet that he uttered these memorable words: "Now, for this cause I know that man is nothing, which thing I had never supposed." Though he was thoroughly overwhelmed to the point of feeling that man is "nothing," yet through this vision, he received abundant reassurance that man is *something*! In fact, the promotion of man's happiness is at the center of God's plans! Clearly, these truths are anything but trivial.

We also learn how Satan came tempting Moses, even begging Moses to worship him. The spiritually experienced Moses was quick to discern the absence of glory surrounding Satan; Moses "could not even look upon God, except his glory should come upon" him and transfigure him. So Moses dispatched Satan, who departed "with a loud voice, and rent upon the earth." Moses actually saw Satan "weeping, and wailing, and gnashing [his] teeth." This is another "plain and precious" insight—especially relevant today when the idea of a devil is cavalierly or comically dismissed as a nonperson and nonfactor in human affairs. Yet he has been a factor more often than we know, such as in this example concerning the Tower of Babel:

> And also it is that same being who put it into the hearts of the people to build a tower sufficiently high that they might get to heaven. And it

> was that same being who led on the people who came from that tower into this land; who spread the works of darkness and abominations over all the face of the land, until he dragged the people down to an entire destruction, and to an everlasting hell. (Helaman 6:28.)

> And they said, Go to, let us build us a city and a tower, whose top may reach unto heaven; and let us make us a name, lest we be scattered abroad upon the face of the whole earth. (Genesis 11:4.)

These added "plain and precious" words tell us who the architect of the tower was and how he caressed mortal egos of his clients for his own purposes. He has not lost that skill.

Even the very voice of God is described to us intriguingly and consistently, representing the variety and beauty of these assorted gems:

> And it came to pass that there came a voice as if it were above the cloud of darkness, saying: Repent ye, repent ye, and seek no more to destroy my servants whom I have sent unto you to declare good tidings.
> And it came to pass when they heard this voice, and beheld that it was not a voice of thunder, neither was it a voice of a great tumultuous noise, but behold, it was a still voice of perfect mildness, as if it had been a whisper, and it did pierce even to the very soul—
> And notwithstanding the mildness of the voice, behold the earth shook exceedingly, and the walls of the prison trembled again, as if it were about to tumble to the earth; and behold the cloud of darkness, which had overshadowed them, did not disperse. (Helaman 5:29-31.)

> And it came to pass that while they were thus conversing one with another, they heard a voice as if it came out of heaven; and they cast their eyes round about, for they understood not the voice which they heard; and it was not a harsh voice, neither was it a loud voice; nevertheless, and notwithstanding it being a small voice it did pierce them that did hear to the center, insomuch that there was no part of their frame that it did not cause to quake; yea, it did pierce them to the very soul, and did cause their hearts to burn. (3 Nephi 11:3.)

It was in the precious vision of Moses upon a mount that the capsulated purpose of God's work was expressed in such splendor: "For behold, this is my work and my glory—to bring to pass the immortality and eternal life of man." (Moses 1:39; compare 2 Nephi 2:26.)

In this same marvelous episode, Moses was told of a time when the recorded words that he provided (which comprise the front portion of the Holy Bible) would, unfortunately, be esteemed "as naught" by many mortals. However, another leader would be raised up, so that the precious words could "be had again among the children of men—among as many as shall believe." (Moses 1:41.) Disbelievers still deflect them, however.

The cross support of the scriptures for one another appears again and again. In connection with Moses' vision on Sinai, we read: "And when Aaron and all the children of Israel saw Moses, behold, the skin of his face shone; and they were afraid to come nigh him." (Exodus 34:30.) Compare these words from the book of Mosiah: "Now it came to pass after Abinadi had spoken these words that the people of king Noah durst not lay their hands on him, for the Spirit of the Lord was upon him; and his face shone with exceeding luster, even as Moses' did while in the mount of Sinai, while speaking with the Lord." (Mosiah 13:5.)

Another biblical translation of this same episode mistakenly said of Moses that "his face was horned"—hence the Michelangelo statue so representing Moses.

Not only do we get from the "other books" of scripture additional information about Joseph and Moses; we also receive information about another very impressive person, Melchizedek. What Joseph Smith gave us in his extensive translation of the fourteenth chapter of Genesis is obviously correlated with that which we receive in the thirteenth chapter of Alma.

Even in the seemingly miscellaneous gospel gems there is plainness and preciousness. If, for instance, we assume there is only ancient relevance concerning the practice and purposes of

priestcraft, we need to be braced by how germane that defini-
tion is for our time. "He commandeth that there shall be no
priestcrafts; for, behold, priestcrafts are that men preach and
set themselves up for a light unto the world, that they may get
gain and praise of the world; but they seek not the welfare of
Zion." (2 Nephi 26:29.) Do we not see such people working
today (minus the label, of course) among the children of men?
Alas, such match the criteria set forth not only as some lead
out in the realm of religion but in the realm of irreligion.

Secularism, too, has its own "priests" and is jealous over its
own "orthodoxy." Those who choose not to follow Him are
sometimes quick to say "Follow me"; they enjoy being a light,
and the accompanying recognition and reward are not
unpleasant.

We see in "these last records," in still other assorted but
useful ways, the careful correlation by the Lord of the prophets
of different dispensations. Nephi, for instance, saw in detail the
end of the world and the winding-up scenes. So at a later time
did John the Beloved. The Lord gave, as it were, exclusive
recording rights to John. (See 1 Nephi 14:15-30.) Nephi was
instructed as follows: "But the things which thou shalt see hereafter thou shalt not write; for the Lord God hath ordained the
apostle of the Lamb of God that he should write them." Then
Nephi added, "And I, Nephi, heard and bear record, that the
name of the apostle of the Lamb was John, according to the
word of the angel." (1 Nephi 14:25, 27.)

Likewise, "these last records" help us to understand better
the specific audiences to whom Jesus gave particular sermons
as well as the sermons themselves:

> And it came to pass that when Jesus had spoken these words unto
> Nephi, and to those who had been called, (now the number of them
> who had been called, and received power and authority to baptize, was
> twelve) and behold, he stretched forth his hand unto the multitude, and
> cried unto them, saying: Blessed are ye if ye shall give heed unto the

words of these twelve whom I have chosen from among you to minister
unto you, and to be your servants; and unto them I have given power
that they may baptize you with water; and after that ye are baptized
with water, behold, I will baptize you with fire and with the Holy
Ghost; therefore blessed are ye if ye shall believe in me and be baptized,
after that ye have seen me and know that I am. (3 Nephi 12:1.)

Thus we see that at times Jesus spoke with exclusivity to the
Twelve apostles and at other times to the multitudes. (See
Matthew 5:1.)

We also encounter most poignant representations of the
feelings of the prophets as they watch their people amid awful
wickedness. Certain of the phrases in an example from the
writings of Mormon are unmistakably individualized—these
are not the sort of phrases a copyist would generate. There is
too much compressed veracity of feeling and authenticity of
experience witnessing to their validity: "And upon the plates of
Nephi I did make a full account of all the wickedness and
abominations; but upon these plates I did forbear to make a
full account of their wickedness and abominations, for behold,
a continual scene of wickedness and abominations has been
before mine eyes ever since I have been sufficient to behold the
ways of man." (Mormon 2:18.)

Observe the candor of this prophet, who had endured
seeing the evil about him and from such a young age; indeed,
since he had been "sufficient to behold the ways of man":

Behold, I had led them, notwithstanding their wickedness I had led
them many times to battle, and had loved them, according to the love
of God which was in me, with all my heart; and my soul had been
poured out in prayer unto my God all the day long for them; nevertheless, it was without faith, because of the hardness of their hearts.
(Mormon 3:12.)

But behold, I was without hope, for I knew the judgments of the
Lord which should come upon them; for they repented not of their
iniquities, but did struggle for their lives without calling upon that Being

who created them. (Mormon 5:2. See also Mormon 2:12-14 for its eloquent description of the "sorrowing of the damned" who would "struggle with the sword for their lives.")

> And it is impossible for the tongue to describe, or for man to write a perfect description of the horrible scene of the blood and carnage which was among the people, both of the Nephites and of the Lamanites; and every heart was hardened, so that they delighted in the shedding of blood continually. (Mormon 4:11.)

Do we not now see such a coarsening about us, whether in the vulgarization of language or in the growing terrorism of our time?

The response of another witness, Moroni, to the ceaseless and senseless slaughter round about him is its own tender verification of validity. Moroni, who gave us so much by way of doctrinal confirmation, clarification, and amplification, is personal rather than doctrinal in these verses; this might well be called his "ore I have none" lamentation:

> And my father also was killed by them, and I even remain alone to write the sad tale of the destruction of my people. But behold, they are gone, and I fulfil the commandment of my father. And whether they will slay me, I know not.
>
> Therefore I will write and hide up the records in the earth; and whither I go it mattereth not.
>
> Behold, my father hath made this record, and he hath written the intent thereof. And behold, I would write it also if I had room upon the plates, but I have not; and ore I have none, for I am alone. My father hath been slain in battle, and all my kinsfolk, and I have not friends nor whither to go; and how long the Lord will suffer that I may live I know not. (Mormon 8:3-5.)

Other prophets also have known similar sorrow and solitude. It was so with diligent and brave Ether, who preached the gospel "from the morning to the going down of the sun."

> And I was about to write more, but I am forbidden; but great and marvelous were the prophecies of Ether; but they esteemed him as

naught, and cast him out; and he hid himself in the cavity of a rock by day, and by night he went forth viewing the things which should come upon the people.

And as he dwelt in the cavity of a rock he made the remainder of this record, viewing the destructions which came upon the people, by night. (Ether 13:13-14.)

Finally, in Ether's time too, the anarchy became absolute: "Now there began to be a war upon all the face of the land, every man with his band fighting for that which he desired." (Ether 13:25.) Destruction produced its own intoxication: "And when the night came they were drunken with anger, even as a man who is drunken with wine; and they slept again upon their swords." (Ether 15:22.)

Preceding the second coming, will there be such similar and widespread violence, disorder, and anarchy again? Yet even in the midst of such destruction, the Lord's purposes unfold, not only generally but individually, as He keeps His individualized promises to His servants.

Almost one whole chapter of Third Nephi is given over to informing us about the Three Nephites, who were translated beings. If we want to know something more about John the Beloved, also a translated being, it is the amplification in the Book of Mormon that tells us about the special mission to which he was called by Jesus—at his own request!

> Jesus saith unto him, If I will that he tarry till I come, what is that to thee? follow thou me. (John 21:22.)

> Therefore, more blessed are ye, for ye shall never taste of death; but ye shall live to behold all the doings of the Father unto the children of men, even until all things shall be fulfilled according to the will of the Father, when I shall come in my glory with the powers of heaven. . . .
> And now I, Mormon, make an end of speaking concerning these things for a time.
> Behold, I was about to write the names of those who were never to taste of death, but the Lord forbade; therefore I write them not, for they are hid from the world.

> But behold, I have seen them, and they have ministered unto me. And behold they will be among the Gentiles, and the Gentiles shall know them not. (3 Nephi 28:24-27.)

There is even a return to that same topic, centuries later,[3] in personal testimony and tender disclosure from Mormon and Moroni:

> And there are none that do know the true God save it be the disciples of Jesus, who did tarry in the land until the wickedness of the people was so great that the Lord would not suffer them to remain with the people; and whether they be upon the face of the land no man knoweth.
>
> But behold, my father and I have seen them, and they have ministered unto us. (Mormon 8:10-11.)
>
> And it was by faith that the three disciples obtained a promise that they should not taste of death; and they obtained not the promise until after their faith. (Ether 12:17.)

Just as we find in the "other books" elaboration concerning the Three Nephites, so we also obtain insights involving matters on a much larger scale, including the most explicit description of a Christian culture and society given in all of holy writ.

What we read in the book of Acts (see Acts 2:41-47) is just enough to be intriguing about those early Christians who "were of one heart and of one soul" and who "had all things common." (Acts 4:32-35.) Much of the same portrait of a people emerges in the Pearl of Great Price, though without the detail we might desire, concerning the City of Enoch, wherein the people there too "were of one heart and one mind, and dwelt in righteousness; and there was no poor among them." (Moses 7:18.)

The exclusive model, however, both as to a glorious spiritual apogee and a lamentable fall, is given to us in the Book of Mormon, in Fourth Nephi.

Synopsis of the People of Nephi

The Rise (A.D. 36 to A.D. 111—about 75 years)

The Church of Christ flourished, and all people were converted. There were population growth, prosperity, and city building. There were fasting, praying, and meeting together oft to hear the word of the Lord. The people kept the commandments they had received from the resurrected Lord, and there were many miracles. This society is described as one in which were found—

> No contentions.
> No disputations.
> Every man dealing justly one with another.
> All things in common.
> Peace and prosperity in the land.
> A love of God in the hearts of the people.
> No envyings, strifes, tumults, whoredoms, lying, murders, or lasciviousness.
> No robbers, murderers, or any "-ites."

"They were in one," "and surely there could not be a happier people."

The Decline (A.D. 111 to A.D. 245—about 134 years)

There was a general peace, but then a small group revolted from the Church, and there began to be "Lamanites" again. The population increased, and there was exceeding prosperity. Other churches were built up and began to deny much of Christ's gospel. False prophets arose, other "ites" (factions) appeared, and the Lamanites were once again taught to hate children of God. Society toward the end of this period deteriorated and is described as one in which were found—

> Pride and attachment to the wearing of costly apparel.
> Goods and substance aplenty but held no more in common.
> Classes and divisions among the people.
> Religious persecution.
> All manner of iniquity.
> Ostentatious church buildings.

"And the more wicked part of the people did wax strong and became exceedingly more numerous than were the people of God."

Later decadence and degradation were described in words like these: "They have lost their love, one towards another.... They are without order and without mercy.... They have become strong in their perversion.... They are without principle, and past feeling." (See Moroni 9. "Past feeling" is a fascinating phrase. See also 1 Nephi 17:45; Ephesians 4:19.)

Sodom and Gomorrah, those sinful cities of the plains, were described thus by Ezekiel:

> Behold, this was the iniquity of thy sister Sodom, pride, fulness of bread, and abundance of idleness was in her and in her daughters, neither did she strengthen the hand of the poor and needy.
>
> And they were haughty, and committed abomination before me: therefore I took them away as I saw good. (Ezekiel 16:49-50.)

What lessons the tides of scriptural history wash to our feet!

Notes

1. Robert J. Matthews, "A Greater Portrayal of the Master," *Ensign*, March 1983, p. 8.
2. Ibid, p. 13.
3. See references concerning John the Revelator in John 21:20-24 and D&C 7, and as a resurrected being in D&C 27:12. Both Elijah and Moses were translated beings on the Mount of Transfiguration (Matthew 17) and appeared later as resurrected beings in the Kirtland Temple (D&C 110).

Chapter 8

The Role of Scripture
in the Latter Days

What should be one's last words about such significance as is found in "these last records"?

Inevitably, one's closing reactions are those of profound appreciation for the vast spiritual treasure that has been given.

Likewise, everlasting gratitude for the reinforcing confirmation about Jesus, the Savior of the world.

And genuine thanksgiving for the elaboration and clarification that these "other books" bring to us concerning the other major messages of the gospel of Jesus Christ.

Similarly, special appreciation for the "plain and precious things" thus given to us, including those that remove otherwise troublesome stumbling blocks.

Heartfelt thanks, too, for the assorted gems contained in "these last records" that aid us so greatly in the daily task of taking up the Christian's cross.

Certainly, too, genuine gratitude for those precious teachings when one needs to pause, at least for a moment, to enjoy the faith—instead of defending the faith.

And so much more!

Yet there is still more over which serious readers can be joyful, for we are permitted to view various prophets as they open the windows of their souls.

What we see is as tender as it is instructive, as reassuring as it is moving. The interweavings we receive in these "other books," therefore, not only involve splendid doctrines and truths but also splendid personalities. We see, in process of time, the sculpturing of souls, and we are thereby counseled, tacitly as well as explicitly, concerning the process that is underway in the sculpturing of our own souls.

We see in these faithful forebears shortfalls, struggles, and strivings, but also immense integrity and far-reaching faith.

And so often we witness the deep gratitude and the genuine empathy of the various prophets as they rejoice, tenderly and individually, as individuals (or whole peoples) are brought closer to the Lord.

> For if we had not come up out of the land of Zarahemla, these our dearly beloved brethren, who have so dearly beloved us, would still have been racked with hatred against us, yea, and they would also have been strangers to God.
>
> And it came to pass that when Ammon had said these words, his brother Aaron rebuked him, saying: Ammon, I fear that thy joy doth carry thee away unto boasting.
>
> But Ammon said unto him: I do not boast in my own strength, nor in my own wisdom; but behold, my joy is full, yea, my heart is brim with joy, and I will rejoice in my God.
>
> Yea, I know that I am nothing; as to my strength I am weak; therefore I will not boast of myself, but I will boast of my God, for in his strength I can do all things; yea, behold, many mighty miracles we have wrought in this land, for which we will praise his name forever. (Alma 26:9-12.)
>
> Now these sons of Mosiah were with Alma at the time the angel first appeared unto him; therefore Alma did rejoice exceedingly to see his brethren; and what added more to his joy, they were still his brethren in the Lord; yea, and they had waxed strong in the knowledge of the truth; for they were men of a sound understanding and they had searched the scriptures diligently, that they might know the word of God. (Alma 17:2.)

How personally these men counseled their loved ones and colleagues!

Just as Paul tutored Timothy (see 1 and 2 Timothy), so it

was with Alma and Corianton (see Alma 39): "And now, my son, I desire that ye should let these things trouble you no more, and only let your sins trouble you, with that trouble which shall bring you down unto repentance." (Alma 42:29.)

The prophets of these other books strove to follow consistently the counsel of Jesus as, by way of illustration, across dispensations and continents, the need to be wise but harmless was heeded. (See Matthew 10:16.) For example, "Ammon being wise, yet harmless, . . . said unto Lamoni: Wilt thou hearken unto my words, if I tell thee by what power I do these things? And this is the thing that I desire of thee." (Alma 18:22.)

Beauty and variety abound, and so does individuality. Not only does the poetry of Jacob bless us, but the graphic words of his colleagues are "no less serviceable" in the cause of truth:

> Now, this was what Ammon desired, for he knew that king Lamoni was under the power of God; he knew that the dark veil of unbelief was being cast away from his mind, and the light which did light up his mind, which was the light of the glory of God, which was a marvelous light of his goodness—yea, this light had infused such joy into his soul, the cloud of darkness having been dispelled, and that the light of everlasting life was lit up in his soul, yea, he knew that this had overcome his natural frame, and he was carried away in God. (Alma 19:6.)

Prophets are too loving to be other than direct when incisive candor is called for: "But Ammon stood forth and said unto him: Behold, thou shalt not slay thy son; nevertheless, it were better that he should fall than thee, for behold, he has repented of his sins; but if thou shouldst fall at this time, in thine anger, thy soul could not be saved." (Alma 20:17.)

It was Paul who advised us to speak "the truth in love," but speak the truth. For such, said he, is essential if we are to grow up spiritually. (Ephesians 4:15.)

There are obvious differences in the language style of various prophets. Some are blunt, others poetic. The contrast is demonstrated in the interesting verses that follow. Both imagery and validity are combined in the first, a lamentation over a group gone wrong. Directness and preciseness are allied in the second, as an ancient prophet writes to those in our age.

> Yea, they are as a wild flock which fleeth from the shepherd, and scattereth, and are driven, and are devoured by the beasts of the forest. (Mosiah 8:21.)

> Behold, I speak unto you as if ye were present, and yet ye are not. But behold, Jesus Christ hath shown you unto me, and I know your doing. (Mormon 8:35.)

We even see understandable wistfulness for another place and time as human nostalgia occasionally overtakes these prophets:

> Oh, that I could have had my days in the days when my father Nephi first came out of the land of Jerusalem, that I could have joyed with him in the promised land; then were his people easy to be entreated, firm to keep the commandments of God, and slow to be led to do iniquity; and they were quick to hearken unto the words of the Lord—
> Yea, if my days could have been in those days, then would my soul have had joy in the righteousness of my brethren.
> But behold, I am consigned that these are my days, and that my soul shall be filled with sorrow because of this the wickedness of my brethren. (Helaman 7:7-9.)

Equally, one living in our period of history could conclude of the remaining years of the twentieth century that "these are my days." But our days can surely be made more manageable and understandable by the beauty, perspective, and power of "these last records."

Could a young man with Joseph Smith's background and education have produced, at age twenty-four, all of the richness and diversity to be found in these added scriptures? Or could certain phrases in the Book of Mormon—especially when these (a sampling of which is below) are put in context with the events they describe—have been originated by him?

One prophet reassured his anxious people who were worried over an approaching army that the Lord "would deliver them": "Therefore they hushed their fears." (Mosiah 23:28.) In this era, are we not likely to see the equivalent need for—and the providing of—such prophetic reassurances to hush needless anxiety?

The spiritual excitement and rejoicing of another prophet, Ammon, was evident as he gloried in the accomplishments and purposes of the Lord: "Behold, my joy is full, yea, my heart is brim with joy." (Alma 26:11.)

The lamentable in-between state of those who can neither take pleasure in sin any longer nor totally repent is aptly described as "the sorrowing of the damned." (Mormon 2:13.) Such an insightful phrase is in obvious contrast to Paul's "godly sorrow" and "sorrow of the world." (See 2 Corinthians 7:10.)

The insensitive machismo of sexually immoral men who, centuries ago, wounded their wives and children by their unchastity created a sorrowful and poignant circumstance; they had "broken the hearts of [their] tender wives and lost the confidence of [their] children, because of [their] bad examples before them." These failing fathers form a portrait in pathos as, among their unloved ones, "many hearts died, pierced with deep wounds." (Jacob 2:35.)

Surely those who have done any pastoral counseling have encountered some who are trapped between two worlds and who, in their misery, mirror "the sorrowing of the damned."

Surely neighbors, friends, confidants, and family members who have seen the contemporary machismo of immoral men in our time have witnessed the broken hearts of wives and the lost confidence of children; physical hearts go on pumping, but, otherwise, many hearts die, "pierced with deep wounds."

Clearly, phrases such as these are not the heart of the Book of Mormon, but how they touch our hearts! Further, these tie us to the hearts and thoughts of those whose blood, sweat, and tears form the spiritual history that comprises "these last records."

From time to time, it is asserted that Joseph Smith was much influenced by the writings of others. That is the way disbelievers have of accounting for the Book of Mormon. Sketchy similarities and unproven influences are merely superficial speculation. Faint parallels in plot and scenery do not even approach the real issue: the glorious substance of the Book of Mormon!

As was said of the Holy Bible, such criticism "is only words about words, and of what use are words about such words as these?"[1]

Moreover, outside holy writ there is *no* available equivalent, for instance, to the definitive declarations of Alma concerning faith. (See Alma 32.) Nor is there even a pastel parallel concerning how Jesus became perfected in His mercy as a part of the great process of the atonement. His empathy and capacity to succor us—in our own sicknesses, temptations, or sins—were demonstrated and perfected in the process of the great atonement. It was therein that He, though sinless, came to know, personally and "according to the flesh," all of that through which we individually pass. (See Alma 7:11-12.)

Undoubtedly, the adversary's frenzied reaction to the coming forth of the Book of Mormon and to "these last records" attesting to the divinity of Jesus Christ plays its part in such scorn as is heaped upon the precious modern scriptures. But just because truth unnerves the miserable one, this is no reason for us mortals to lose our nerve or our capacity to rejoice over receiving greater portions of Jesus' gospel—now blessedly verified, amplified, and clarified. Still, there are those critics who insist on leaping to wrong conclusions, as if that were their only form of exercise.

Actually, the last word about "these last records" is, in fact, that they are not the last records. There is, happily, other scripture yet to come!

Therefore, those who have assumed a posture of rejection toward those "plain and precious things" which have come forth will be in that same provincial posture as still more witnessing scriptures come forth. All of this a merciful God gives to His children to establish *convincingly,* as never before in human history, that Jesus is the very Christ and Redeemer of the world.

Of that glorious fact, this author bears his witness in apostolic authority.

Note
1. Richard L. Purtill, *C. S. Lewis's Case for the Christian Faith* (San Francisco: Harper & Row, 1981), p. 53.

Index